KA
From Zero!

George Trombley
Yukari Takenaka

Visit our website to meet other students in the chat room or forums.

JapaneseFromZero.com

Distributed worldwide by:
From Zero, LLC
10624 S. Eastern Ave. #A769,
Henderson, NV 89052.

First edition, Dec, 2014

Questions, Comments, Wholesale?
book@learnfromzero.com

KANA From Zero!

About this book

Introduction

❑ **Welcome to *Kana From Zero!***
Learning to write Japanese can be intimidating at first, but don't worry! Our method is designed to lead you step-by-step through the basics of hiragana, katakana, and even kanji.

❑ **Japanese characters**
WHAT ARE THESE STRANGE LETTERS? The Japanese language uses a set of symbols called *hiragana* (to spell Japanese words), *katakana* (to spell foreign words), and *kanji* (to represent entire words or names). This book will teach you hiragana followed by katakana character by characer to gradually build up your understanding and familiarity.

Until you can read hiragana, this book will use *ro–maji* (Japanese words spelled with Roman letters), but as each lesson progresses, we will continually substitute them with the hiragana you've learned. By the end of this book, you will be able to read and write hiragana and katakana!

❑ **Japanese punctuation facts**
HERE ARE SOME QUICK FACTS about Japanese writing to help you get started.

UPPERCASE/LOWERCASE
There are no upper and lower cases in Japanese. In English, we learn to write both *A* and *a*, but in Japanese, あ is always あ.

PERIODS
Japanese periods are small circles instead of dots.
Kore wa hon desu. → in hiragana becomes → これは ほんです。

How this book works

This book uses *Japanese From Zero's* PROGRESSIVE SYSTEM of teaching. As you learn new hiragana, we will immediately replace the roman letters (ro–maji) with the hiragana you have just learned. For example, after you learn あ (which sounds like "ah") we will mix it into the example words.

English	Before	After	After book
you	anata	あ nata	あなた
dog	inu	い nu	いぬ
house	ie	いえ	いえ
mother	okaasan	お ka あ san	おかあさん

About the authors

Author George Trombley is a professional Japanese interpreter who over the past 16 years has interpreted at corporations such as Microsoft, Motorola, NTT DoCoMo, Varian Medical, and in countries throughout North America, Europe, Asia and the Middle East.

George Trombley and his wife Yukari Takenaka formed a Japanese Language School in 1998 and since then, the live classroom courses have formed the basis for the *Japanese From Zero!* textbook series and the YesJapan.com interactive language learning website.

Write in this book!

From Zero! is designed to be an interactive workbook where you can take personal notes, add new words or phrases of your own, and develop your writing from hopeless/crazy/illegible to expert-level.

Every time you write in this book, you're making your connection to Japanese a little bit stronger - we guarantee it!

Ganbatte kudasai!
George Trombley
Yukari Takenaka

Pronunciation Guide & The Basics

Why Learn Hiragana and Katakana?

All of your life you have been reading the alphabet a certain way. You have learned that the letter combination "TO" sounds like the number 2. This instinct may be hard to overcome at first.

In Japanese, "TO" is read as "TOW". If you read this like you were taught in grade school your Japanese accent would be pretty bad! Learning the hiragana and katakana solves this problem.

Before you can learn hiragana and katakana, you will need to know how Japanese is represented in the Roman alphabet. This lesson will teach you how Japanese is pronounced. Let's get started!

The Japanese Writing Systems

There are three Japanese writing systems:
- hiragana (pronounced "hear-uh-gah-nah")
- katakana (pronounced "kah-tah-kah-nah")
- kanji (pronounced "kahn-jee")

Kanji are Chinese characters, and each one has a specific meaning. Many kanji have multiple meanings and can be read different ways. Hiragana and katakana are phonetic characters derived from the more complicated kanji. They each represent a sound and do not have meaning by themselves.

The three writing systems are used together to write Japanese. Hiragana and kanji are used together to form all Japanese words. Katakana is mostly used to represent words of foreign origin or any word that was not originally Japanese. In daily life the combination of these three systems, plus roman letters called "ro–maji", are used in all types of media.

Japanese Pronunciation

Anyone can sound great in Japanese. Although English is made up of over a thousand possible sounds, Japanese has many less. A little over a hundred sounds are all you need to speak Japanese.

For this reason, it is much easier for English-speaking people to learn natural Japanese pronunciation than it is for Japanese speakers to learn natural English pronunciation. With just a few exceptions, Japanese sounds are based on the following five vowel sounds:

❑ Normal vowels

These sounds are short and simple, with no glide or lengthening.

Roman Letter	Sounds Like	Example
a	**ah** as in f**a**ther	**a**kai (red)
i	**ee** as in s**ee**	**i**nochi (life)
u	**oo** as in z**oo**	**u**ma (horse)
e	**eh** as in m**e**n	**e**bi (shrimp)
o	**oh** as in b**o**at	**o**toko (man)

Now let's look at some more sounds. Use the same pronunciation as above for the sound sets listed below.

ka, ki, ku, ke, ko	sa, shi, su, se, so	pa, pi, pu, pe, po
ga, gi, gu, ge, go	na, ni, nu, ne, no	ba, bi, bu, be, bo

The following phonetic sounds are based on the "normal vowel" sounds listed above. The only difference is how the sound starts.

Roman Letter	Sounds Like	Example
ka	kah	**ka** (mosquito)
shi	shee	**shi**ru (to know)
tsu	tsoo	**tsu**ru (crane bird)
ne	neh	**ne**ko (cat)
po	poh	tan**po**po (dandelion)

❏ Double vowels

To display a lengthened vowel, this book will use A, I, U, E, or O after the vowel sound that is to be lengthened. This style mimics how lengthening is done when writing in hiragana and katakana.

Roman Letters	Sound	Example
aa, a–	**ah** as in f**a**ther	ok**aa**san (mother)
ii, i–	**ee** as in s**ee**	oj**ii**san (grandfather)
uu, u–	**oo** as in z**oo**	zu**tsuu** (headache)
ei, ee, e–	**eh** as in m**e**n	on**ee**san (older sister)
ou, oo, o–	**oh** as in b**oa**t	**mou**fu (blanket)

Words that are written in katakana often use a "–" as the "lengthener" instead of a repeating vowel (shown above). You'll learn more about katakana after the hiragana section.

Example Words (with double vowels)

kyouts<u>uu</u>	common	ot<u>ou</u>san	father
sat<u>ou</u>	sugar	ob<u>aa</u>san	grandmother
h<u>ei</u>wa	peace	sens<u>ou</u>	war
yasash<u>ii</u>	kind	isogash<u>ii</u>	busy

❏ Long versus short sounds

The meaning of a Japanese word can be changed by lengthening just one syllable.

Examples

ie	house
<u>ii</u>e	no
obasan	aunt
ob<u>aa</u>san	grandmother
ojisan	uncle
oj<u>ii</u>san	grandfather

❏ Double consonants

Some Japanese words use double consonant sounds. Double consonants such as 'kk', 'pp', 'tt', and 'cch' must be stressed more than a single consonant to show the correct meaning of a word.

> **Examples**
>
> | | |
> |---|---|
> | roku | number six |
> | ro<u>kk</u>u | rock (music) |
> | | |
> | uta | a song |
> | u<u>tt</u>a | sold (past tense verb) |
> | | |
> | mata | again |
> | ma<u>tt</u>a | waited (past tense verb) |

Lesson 1: Hiragana あいうえお

Some History れきし

Hiragana was created by a Buddhist monk over 1200 years ago (AD 774-835). At that time women were not allowed to learn the very intricate kanji. After hiragana was introduced, women were able to express themselves in the written form. It is due to hiragana that women authored many of the first published works in Japan.

Hiragana character samples

あ か さ た な は ま や ら わ ん

Katakana was created by using portions of kanji, while the more rounded hiragana was created by simplifying kanji. Children learn hiragana first, then katakana, and finally kanji.

Katakana character samples

ア カ サ タ ナ ハ マ ヤ ラ ワ ン

In 2010 the Japanese Ministry of Education added to the original 1,945 commonly used kanji, called the *Joyou Kanji*, upping the total required kanji to 2,136. By the 6th grade, the average Japanese student knows half of the *Joyou Kanji*.

Kanji character samples

安 加 左 太 奈 波 末 也 良 和 毛

The goal ゴール

When you complete the hiragana section you will be able to read and write the hiragana symbols shown below + the combined hiragana.

46 standard hiragana

25 altered hiragana

Writing Basics かくときの きほん

❑ What is a stroke?

A stroke begins when the pen (or any other writing device) comes in contact with the paper. The stroke ends when the pen separates from the paper.

❑ Why use brushes to write?

Traditionally, Japanese was written with brushes. This book – and almost any book that teaches Japanese writing – uses the brush-written style for the Japanese characters. The brush-written style best represents how the characters should be written.

❑ Different types of brush strokes

There are three types of strokes. For ease of understanding we have named them *fade out*, *dead stop* and *bounce fade*. Whether writing with a brush, pen, or pencil, make sure that you pay attention to the stroke type. This will ensure that your writing is neat and proper.

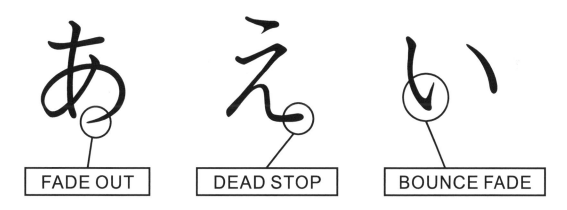

| FADE OUT | DEAD STOP | BOUNCE FADE |

If your teacher is Japanese you might hear the Japanese names of the stroke types:

Fade out – harai (harau)
Dead stop – tome (tomeru)
Bounce fade – hane (haneru)

New Hiragana あたらしい ひらがな

The first five hiragana to learn are listed below. Notice the different stroke types. Be sure to learn the correct stroke order and stroke type.

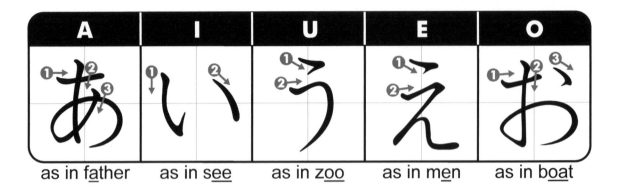

as in f<u>a</u>ther   as in s<u>ee</u>   as in z<u>oo</u>   as in m<u>e</u>n   as in b<u>oa</u>t

Various Styles スタイル

Write each symbol as neatly as you can in the writing practice section, then compare it to the different versions below.

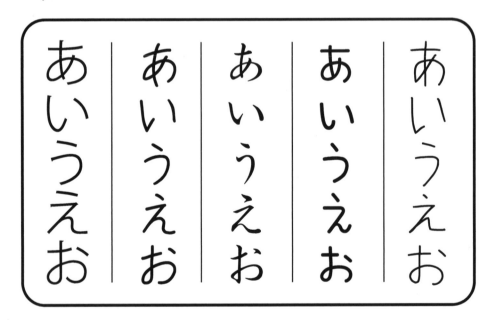

❏ **The importance of the various styles**

It is important to know what is allowed when writing. Remember that there are small differences between how the characters will look when writing with a brush and writing with a pen or pencil.

Writing Points かくポイント

❑ The difference between あ (a) and お (o)

Be careful not to mix up あ and お. The second stroke of あ is curved while the second stroke for お is straight until the loop.

more curved than お and not connected to the loop.

straighter than あ and connected to the loop.

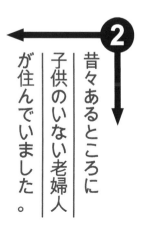

❑ Writing left-to-right and top-to-bottom

Before World War II, most Japanese publications were written from top to bottom as shown in style 2. In modern Japan, the style used is based solely on design choice, and in some cases (such as writing an e-mail) only style 1 is possible. Many Japanese writing books for children will use style 2. *From Zero!* contains only style 1.

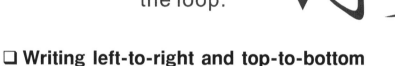

1 昔々あるところに
子供のいない老婦人が
住んでいました。

2 昔々あるところに
子供のいない老婦人
が住んでいました。

Writing Practice れんしゅう

Trace the light gray characters, then write each character six times.

a	あ	あ						
i	い	い						
u	う	う						
e	え	え						
o	お	お						

Word Practice ことばの れんしゅう

Fill in the appropriate hiragana in the blanks for each word.

1. ___ka___san (mother)
   o   a

2. ___ ___ (house)
   i   e

3. ___to___san (father)
   o   u

4. ___ka ___ (red)
   a   i

5. ___mo___to (younger sister)
   i   u

6. ka___ (to buy)
       u

7. ___sagi (rabbit)
   u

8. ___npitsu (pencil)
   e

9. ___ne___san (older sister)
   o   e

10. ___moshiro___ (interesting)
    o   i

11.___su (chair)
    i

12. ___kiru (to wake up)
    o

Words You Can Write かける ことば

Write the following words using the hiragana that you just learned. This is a great way to increase your Japanese vocabulary.

a painting

え

good

いい

nephew

おい

love

あい

ray fish

えい

no

いいえ

many

おおい

to meet

あう

up

う	え								

to say

い	う								

house

い	え								

blue

あ	う								

Hiragana Matching ひらがな マッチング

Connect the dots between each hiragana and the correct ro–maji.

お・   ・a

う・   ・o

え・   ・u

い・   ・e

あ・   ・i

Everyday Hiragana Words にちじょうの ことば

あ kachan
baby

い nu
dog

う shi
cow

ka え ru
frog

お koru
to get mad

う chu う
space

Answer Key こたえ あわせ

No one likes to flip to the back of the book. Here are the answers.

❏ Lesson 1: Word practice

1. お ka あ san
2. いえ
3. お to う san
4. あ ka い
5. い mo う to
6. ka う
7. う sagi
8. え npitsu
9. お ne え san
10. お moshiro い
11. い su
12. お kiru

❏ Lesson 1: Hiragana matching

お ——————— a
う ——————— o
え ——————— u
い ——————— e
あ ——————— i

Hiragana Practice Sheet れんしゅう

Lesson 2: Hiragana かきくけこ

New Hiragana あたらしい ひらがな

Correct stroke order will mean neater characters when writing quickly.

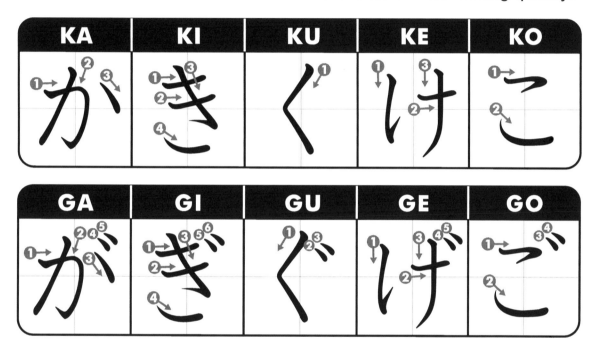

Various Styles スタイル

Write each symbol as neatly as you can, then compare it to the different versions below.

かきくけこ　かきくけこ　かきくけこ　かきくけこ　かきくけこ

がぎぐげご　がぎぐげご　がぎぐげご　がぎぐげご　がぎぐげご

Writing Points かくポイント

❑ **The dakuten**

The only difference between *ka ki ku ke ko* and *ga gi gu ge go* are the last two small strokes up in the right hand corner. Those strokes are called *dakuten*. You will see them often in future lessons.

❑ **Writing が (ga) the correct way**

When adding *dakuten* to か (ka) to make it が (ga), make sure that they are shorter than the third stroke. The third stroke of が should always be longer than the *dakuten*.

が	**INCORRECT** (dakuten are too long)
が	**INCORRECT** (dakuten are too short)
が	**CORRECT**

❑ **The different versions of き (ki)**

There are two versions of *ki*. It is your choice which version you use. You will see both in Japan depending on font or style choice.

き	This version has four strokes and is very common when writing. Many Japanese people write using this version.
き	This version has combined the third and fourth strokes into one stroke. It is very common in printed text such as books and magazines.

Writing Practice れんしゅう

First trace the gray characters, then write each character six times.

ka	か	か						
ki	き	き						
ku	く	く						
ke	け	け						
ko	こ	こ						

ga	が	が						
gi	ぎ	ぎ						
gu	ぐ	ぐ						
ge	げ	げ						
go	ご	ご						

Word Practice ことばの れんしゅう

Fill in the appropriate hiragana in the blanks for each word.

1. ___いro   (yellow)
   ki

2. ___ ___   (to listen)
   ki ku

3. ___minari   (lightning)
   ka

4. ___う___n   (air force)
   ku gu

5. ___ ___   (moss)
   ko ke

6. い___   (to go)
   ku

7. ___mushi   (caterpillar)
   ke

8. ___う___う   (airport)
   ku ko

9. ___nいro   (silver color)
   gi

10. ___n'ni___   (muscle)
    ki   ku

11. ___ ___   (afternoon)
    go go

12. ___おri   (ice)`
    ko

Words You Can Write かける ことば

Write the following words using the hiragana that you just learned. This is a great way to increase your Japanese vocabulary.

tree

き											

to write

か	く										

squid

い	か										

key

| か | ぎ | | | | | | | | | |

face

| か | お | | | | | | | | | |

shell

| か | い | | | | | | | | | |

red

| あ | か | | | | | | | | | |

afternoon, PM

| ご | ご | | | | | | | | | |

air

| く | う | き | | | | | | |

foreign country

| が | い | こ | く | | | | |

big

| お | お | き | い | | | |

airport

| く | う | こ | う | | | |

Hiragana Matching ひらがな マッチング

Connect the dots between each hiragana and the correct ro–maji.

き・	・i
い・	・go
く・	・ka
か・	・ki
え・	・ku
ご・	・ke
け・	・e

Everyday Hiragana Words にちじょうの ことば

tsu き
the moon

けい ta い denwa
cell phone

かぎ
key

cho き n ba こ
safe, piggy
bank

かく
to write

su いか
watermelon

Answer Key こたえ あわせ

❑ Lesson 2: Word Practice

1. きい ro
2. きく
3. か minari
4. くうぐ n
5. こけ
6. いく
7. け mushi
8. くうこう
9. ぎ n い ro
10. き n'ni く
11. ごご
12. こお ri

❑ Lesson 2: Hiragana matching

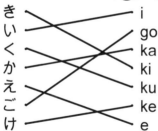

き   i
い   go
く   ka
か   ki
え   ku
ご   ke
け   e

Hiragana Practice Sheet れんしゅう

Lesson 3: Hiragana さしすせそ

New Hiragana あたらしい ひらがな

Correct stroke order will mean neater characters when writing quickly.

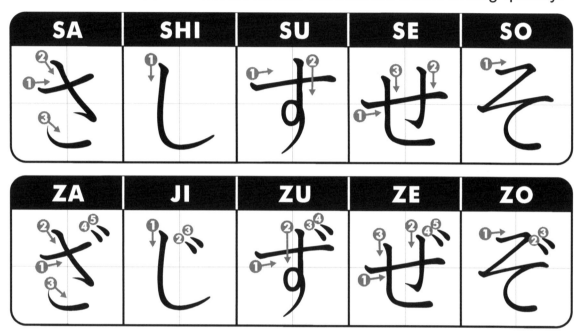

Various Styles スタイル

Write each symbol as neatly as you can, then compare it to the different versions below.

Writing Points かくポイント

❑ The different versions of さ (sa) and そ (so)

You may have noticed in the *Various Styles* section of this lesson that there are two versions of *sa* and *so*. You can write whichever version you choose, so long as it is legible.

Different versions of さ (sa)	
さ	This version has three strokes and is very common when writing. Most Japanese people use this version when writing.
さ	This version has combined the second and third strokes into one stroke. It is very common in printed text.

Different versions of そ (so)	
そ	This version has two strokes and is common when writing. Many Japanese people write using this version.
そ	This version similar to version above except that the first and second stroke are touching.
そ	This version has only one stroke and is very common in printed text. It is also acceptable for writing.

Writing Practice れんしゅう

First trace the gray characters, then write each character six times.

sa	さ	さ					
shi	し	し					
su	す	す					
se	せ	せ					
so	そ	そ					

za	ざ	ざ					
ji	じ	じ					
zu	ず	ず					
ze	ぜ	ぜ					
zo	ぞ	ぞ					

Word Practice ことばの れんしゅう

Fill in the appropriate hiragana in the blanks for each word.

1. mura___き (purple)
   sa

2. ___ ___ (to point)
   sa su

3. ___ro (white)
   shi

4. ___tsugyo う (graduation)
   so

5. ___ ___ (sushi)
   su shi

6. ___か n (time)
   ji

7. ___ru (monkey)
   sa

8. お___い___n (grandfather)
   ji   sa

9. あ___ (sweat)
   se

10. あ n___n (safety)
    ze

11. ___う (elephant)
    zo

12. げ n___い (currently, at present)
    za

Words You Can Write かける ことば

Write the following words using the hiragana that you just learned.

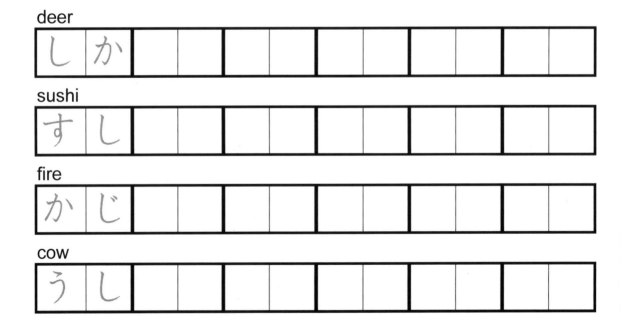

deer
しか

sushi
すし

fire
かじ

cow
うし

numbers / amount

| か | ず | | | | | | | | | | |

legs / feet

| あ | し | | | | | | | | | | |

chair

| い | す | | | | | | | | | | |

like

| す | き | | | | | | | | | | |

slow / late

| お | そ | い | | | | | | | |

number

| す | う | じ | | | | | | | |

family

| か | ぞ | く | | | | | | | |

world

| せ | か | い | | | | | | | |

watermelon

| す | い | か | | | | | | | |

cool (temperature)

| す | ず | し | い | | | | | | |

Hiragana Matching ひらがな マッチング

Connect the dots between each hiragana and the correct ro–maji.

<table>
<tr><td>す ·</td><td>· za</td></tr>
<tr><td>し ·</td><td>· su</td></tr>
<tr><td>え ·</td><td>· ku</td></tr>
<tr><td>こ ·</td><td>· shi</td></tr>
<tr><td>ざ ·</td><td>· i</td></tr>
<tr><td>あ ·</td><td>· e</td></tr>
<tr><td>く ·</td><td>· ko</td></tr>
<tr><td>い ·</td><td>· a</td></tr>
</table>

Everyday Hiragana Words にちじょうの ことば

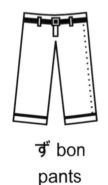

ず bon
pants

し nbun
newspaper

tsu くえ
desk

さ mu い
cold

wa くせい
planet

すし
sushi

Answer Key こたえ あわせ

❑ Lesson 3: Word practice

1. mura さき
2. さす
3. し ro
4. そ tsugyo う
5. すし
6. じか n
7. さ ru
8. おじいさ n
9. あせ
10. あ n ぜ n
11. ぞう
12. げ n ざい

❑ Lesson 3: Hiragana matching

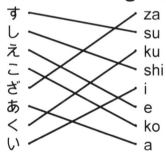

す — za
し — su
え — ku
こ — shi
ざ — i
あ — e
く — ko
い — a

Hiragana Practice Sheet れんしゅう

Lesson 4: Hiragana たちつてと

New Hiragana あたらしい ひらがな

Correct stroke order will mean neater characters when writing quickly.

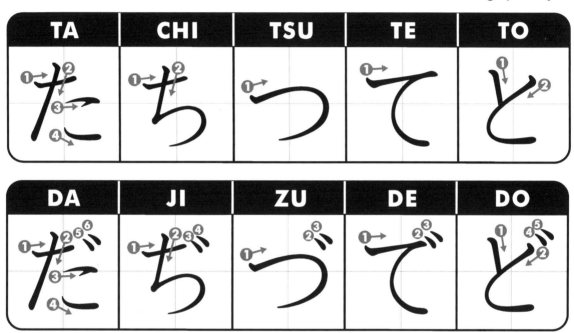

Various Styles スタイル

Write each symbol as neatly as you can, then compare it to the different versions below.

たちってと

たちってと

たちってと

たちってと

たちってと

だぢづでど

だぢづでど

だぢづでど

だぢづでど

だぢづでど

Writing Points かく ポイント

❑ The double consonants

The double consonants (*kk, pp, tt, cch*) are stressed with a slight pause before the consonant. To represent them in hiragana, a small つ is used.* The small つ is always placed in front of the hiragana that needs to be doubled.

> **Examples**
>
> | school | gakkou | がっこう |
> |---|---|---|
> | magazine | zasshi | ざっし |
> | postage stamp | kitte | きって |

* Write the つ smaller than normal to avoid confusion with normal つ.

❑ The double consonant sound analysis

If you look at the sound wave for a word that has a double consonant, you will see a pause or visible space before the consonant. Look at the two samples below:

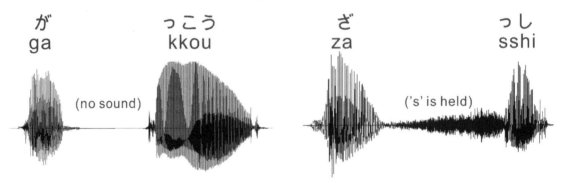

が	っこう	ざ	っし
ga	kkou	za	sshi

(no sound)   ('s' is held)

❑ Which version of *zu* and *ji* should be used?

There are two versions of *zu* and *ji*. The first set is in Lesson 3. ず and じ are more commonly used. づ and ぢ are used in only a few words, such as は na ぢ (nosebleed) and つづく (to continue). If you're not sure about what version to use, try ず and じ and 90% of the time you will be correct.

❑ The つ sound

To say つ, start with the "TS" sound of "BOOTS" then add an う sound.

Writing Practice れんしゅう

First trace the gray characters, then write each character six times.

ta	た	た						
chi	ち	ち						
tsu	つ	つ						
te	て	て						
to	と	と						

da	だ	だ						
ji	ぢ	ぢ						
zu	づ	づ						
de	で	で						
do	ど	ど						

Word Practice ことばの れんしゅう

Fill in the appropriate hiragana in the blanks for each word.

1. wa___し   (me, I)
      ta

2. ___ ___   (free, no charge)
   ta   da

3. ___ ___   (to stand)
   ta   tsu

4. ___ ___ぜ n   (all of a sudden)
   to   tsu

5. ___ ___mu   (to shrink)
   chi   ji

6. ___ ___ ___う   (to help)
   te   tsu   da

7. い___い   (it hurts, ouch)
      ta

8. お ___うさ n   (father)
       to

9. hana___   (nose bleed)
         ji

10. いき___mari   (dead end)
          do

11.___nwa   (telephone)
   de

12. ___ ___く   (to reach, arrive)
   to   do

Words You Can Write かける ことば

Write the following words using the hiragana that you just learned.

free

た	だ								

next

つ	ぎ								

map

ち	ず								

corner

かど

map

ちず

my father

ちち

to stand

たつ

poison

どく

magazine

ざっし

postage stamp

きって

hot

あつい

far

とおい

to deliver

と	ど	く									

continuation

つ	づ	き									

physical education

た	い	い	く							

Hiragana Matching ひらがな マッチング

Connect the dots between each hiragana and the correct ro–maji.

て ·   · tsu

つ ·   · da

さ ·   · chi

ち ·   · te

す ·   · u

ぢ ·   · ji

う ·   · sa

だ ·   · su

Everyday Hiragana Words にちじょうの ことば

で n し renji

microwave oven

hon だ na

bookshelf

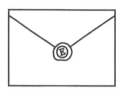

fu うとう

envelope

て

hand

た ma ご

eggs

くつした

socks

Answer Key こたえ あわせ

❑ Lesson 4: Word practice

1. wa たし
2. ただ
3. たつ
4. とつぜ n
5. ちぢ mu
6. てつだう
7. いたい
8. おとうさ n
9. hana ぢ
10. いきど mari
11. で nwa
12. とどく

❑ Lesson 4: Hiragana matching

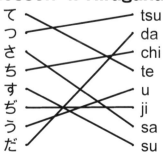

て — tsu
っ — da
さ — chi
ち — te
す — u
ぢ — ji
う — sa
だ — su

Hiragana Practice Sheet れんしゅう

Lesson 5: Hiragana なにぬねの

New Hiragana あたらしい ひらがな

Correct stroke order will mean neater characters when writing quickly.

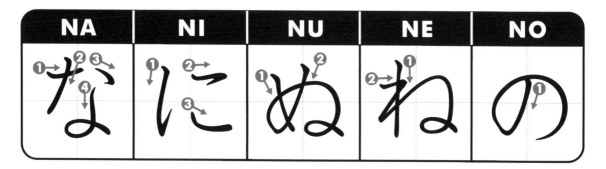

NA	NI	NU	NE	NO

Various Styles スタイル

Write each symbol as neatly as you can, then compare it to the different versions below.

Writing Practice れんしゅう

First trace the gray characters, then write each character six times.

na	な	な						
ni	に	に						
nu	ぬ	ぬ						
ne	ね	ね						
no	の	の						

Word Practice ことばの れんしゅう

Fill in the appropriate hiragana in the blanks for each word.

1. ___つ (summer)
   na

2. ___hon (Japan)
   ni

3. ___こ (cat)
   ne

4. yo___か (middle of the night)
   na

5. ___mu (to drink)
   no

6. ___ru (to sleep, to go to bed)
   ne

7. ___ ___ (what?)
   na ni

8. ___いぐ rumi (stuffed animal)
   nu

9. ___がい (bitter tasting)
   ni

10. お___えさ n (older sister)
    ne

11. ___ぐ (to take off clothes)
    nu

12. ___ru (to ride)
    no

Words You Can Write かける ことば

Write the following words using the hiragana that you just learned.

what?

な	に								

cat

ね	こ								

seven (7)

な	な								

west

に	し								

summer

な	つ								

fever

ね	つ								

dog

い	ぬ								

throat

の	ど								

crab

か	に								

rainbow

| に | じ | | | | | | | | | | |

meat

| に | く | | | | | | | | | | |

inside

| な | か | | | | | | | | | | |

brain

| の | う | | | | | | | | | | |

you

| あ | な | た | | | | | | | | |

diary

| に | っ | き | | | | | | | | |

kitten

| こ | ね | こ | | | | | | | | |

lukewarm, tepid

| ぬ | く | い | | | | | | | | |

Hiragana Matching ひらがな マッチング

Connect the dots between each hiragana and the correct ro–maji.

な・	・no
の・	・ni
か・	・ta
す・	・na
ぬ・	・ka
ね・	・nu
に・	・ne
た・	・su

Everyday Hiragana Words にちじょうの ことば

いぬ
dog

ながい
long

に wa と ri
chicken

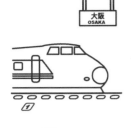

の ru

to ride

ぬ ru

to paint

ねこ

cat

Answer Key こたえ あわせ

❑ Lesson 5: Word practice

1. なつ
2. に hon
3. ねこ
4. yo なか
5. の mu
6. ね ru
7. なに
8. ぬいぐ rumi
9. にがい
10. おねえさ n
11. ぬぐ
12. の ru

❑ Lesson 5: Hiragana matching

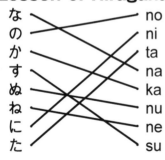

な	no
の	ni
か	ta
す	na
ぬ	ka
ね	nu
に	ne
た	su

Lesson 6: Hiragana はひふへほ

New Hiragana あたらしい ひらがな

Correct stroke order will mean neater characters when writing quickly.

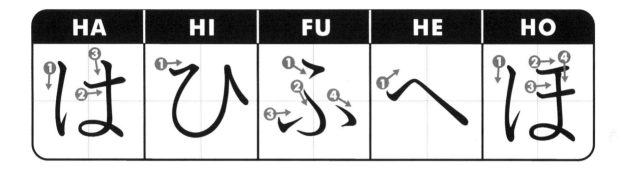

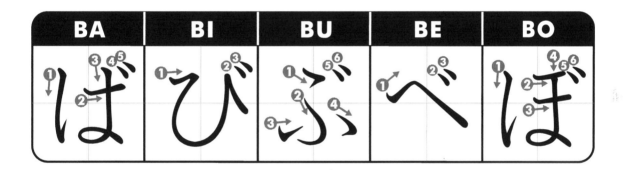

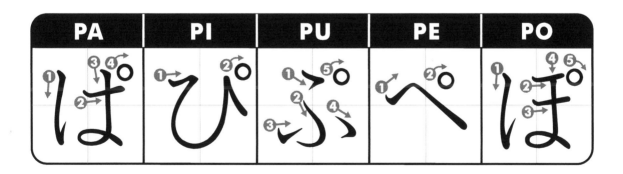

Various Styles スタイル

Write each symbol as neatly as you can, then compare it to the different versions below.

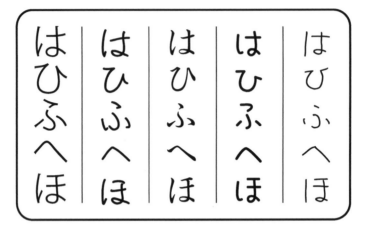

Writing Points かくポイント

❑ What is that circle?

The *pa pi pu pe po* hiragana are made by adding a circle in the area where *dakuten* normally would go. The circle should be written clockwise and is always the last stroke. Most Japanese people refer to this as simply *maru*, which means "circle." The official name for it is *handakuten*.

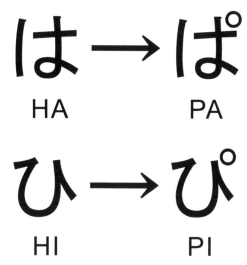

は→ぱ
HA   PA

ひ→ぴ
HI   PI

❑ Why isn't ふ written as *HU*?

Kana From Zero! represents ふ as *FU* instead of *HU* in ro–maji. Japanese people will sometimes represent ふ as *HU* in ro–maji, however, the pronunciation of ふ is closer to *FU*. The F sound in ふ should be voiced softer than the F sound in an English word.

❑ The easy way to write ふ (fu)

ふ tends to be difficult to write, but there is an easy way: connect the first and second stroke into what looks like a number "3."

The 3 Version   Actual Font Versions

Writing Practice れんしゅう

First trace the gray characters, then write each character six times.

ha	は	は						
hi	ひ	ひ						
fu	ふ	ふ						
he	へ	へ						
ho	ほ	ほ						

ba	ば	ば						
bi	び	び						
bu	ぶ	ぶ						
be	べ	べ						
bo	ぼ	ぼ						

pa	ぱ	ぱ						
pi	ぴ	ぴ						
pu	ぶ	ぶ						
pe	ぺ	ぺ						
po	ぽ	ぽ						

Special Usage とくべつな つかいかた

❑ **The topic marker は (wa)**

A topic marker in Japanese identifies the subject of a sentence.
The topic marker "wa" is written using the は (ha) character and can
never be written using the わ (wa) character. In all other situations,
は (ha) is always read as "ha."

Example Sentences
1. あなたは (wa) だ re ですか。
   Who are you?

2. Banana は (wa) きい ro です。
   Bananas are yellow.

❑ **The direction marker へ (e)**

The direction marker "e" is written using the へ (he) character and
can never be written using the え (e) character. In all other
situations, へ (he) is always read as "he."

Example Sentences

1. がっこうへ (e) いき ma す。
   I am going towards (to) school.

2. とう kyo うへ (e) いき ma す。
   I am going towards (to) Tokyo.

Word Practice ことばの れんしゅう

Fill in the appropriate hiragana in the blanks for each word.

1. ___ru   (spring)
   ha

2. ___ru ご___n   (lunch)
   hi   ha

3. ___yu   (winter)
   fu

4. ___い wa   (peace)
   he

5. え___n   (picture book)
   ho

6. が n___ru   (to do your best)
   ba

7. ___な___   (fireworks)
   ha   bi

8. か mi___く ro   (paper bag)
   bu

9. ___と me___re   (love at first sight)
   hi   bo

10. く ra___ru   (to compare)
    be

11. ___ ___な   (electric spark)
    hi   ba

12. え n___つ   (pencil)
    pi

Words You Can Write かける ことば

Write the following words using the hiragana that you just learned.

chopsticks, bridge

は	し									

star (in sky)

ほ	し									

lid, top

ふ	た									

belly button

へ	そ									

pigeon, dove

は	と									

pig

ぶ	た									

person

ひ	と									

to dry

ほ	す									

fat

し	ぼ	う								

tail

し	っ	ぽ									

tofu (soy bean)

と	う	ふ									

leaf

は	っ	ぱ									

cheeks

ほ	っ	ぺ									

hat

ぼ	う	し									

ticket

き	っ	ぷ									

fireworks

は	な	び									

tall person, bean pole

の	っ	ぽ									

first love

は	つ	こ	い						

mistake

し	っ	ぱ	い						

Hiragana Matching ひらがな マッチング

Connect the dots between each hiragana and the correct ro–maji.

ふ ·	· pi
ぺ ·	· pe
ぜ ·	· bo
ぼ ·	· gi
は ·	· fu
た ·	· ze
ぴ ·	· ta
ぎ ·	· ha

Everyday Hiragana Words にちじょうの ことば

ひ sho

secretary

ふく ro う

owl

おばけ

monster

ほうたい
bandage

はし ru
to run

てっぽう
pistol, gun

Answer Key こたえ あわせ

❏ Lesson 6: Word Practice

1. は ru
2. ひ ru ごは n
3. ふ yu
4. へい wa
5. えほ n
6. が n ば ru
7. はなび
8. か mi ぶく ro
9. ひと me ぼ re
10. く ra べ ru
11. ひばな
12. え n ぴつ

❏ Lesson 6: Hiragana matching

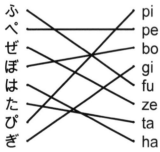

ふ   pi
ぺ   pe
ぜ   bo
ぼ   gi
は   fu
た   ze
ぴ   ta
ぎ   ha

Lesson 7: Hiragana まみむめも

New Hiragana あたらしい ひらがな

Correct stroke order will mean neater characters when writing quickly.

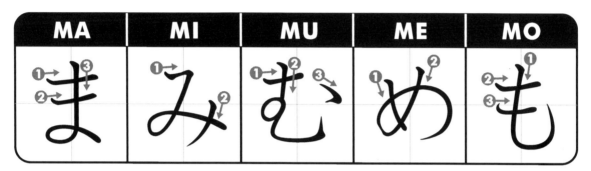

Various Styles スタイル

Write each symbol as neatly as you can, then compare it to the different versions below.

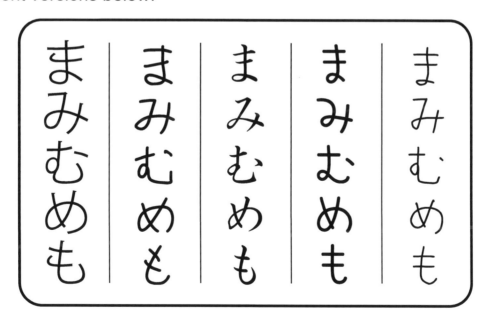

Writing Practice れんしゅう

First trace the gray characters, then write each character six times.

ma	ま	ま						
mi	み	み						
mu	む	む						
me	め	め						
mo	も	も						

Word Practice ことばの れんしゅう

Fill in the appropriate hiragana in the blanks for each word.

1. ___ri (forest)
   mo

2. ___ ___じ (maple leaf)
   mo mi

3. ___ri (impossible)
   mu

4. ___だつ (to stand out)
   me

5. ___ru (to see, to watch)
   mi

6. ___がね (eye glasses)
   me

7. たべ___の (food)
   mo

8. ___ ___ru (to protect)
   ma mo

9. の＿＿＿＿の (a drink)
    mi mo

10. ＿＿しあつい (humid)
     mu

11. ＿＿ほう (magic)
   ma

12. ＿＿＿＿ず (earthworm)
    mi mi

Words You Can Write かける ことば

Write the following words using the hiragana that you just learned.

window

まど								

peach

もも								

miso, bean paste

みそ								

insect

むし								

hair, god, paper

かみ								

no good

だめ								

store

みせ								

cicada, locust

せみ

head

あたま

nick name

あだな

serious

まじめ

sashimi

さしみ

son

むすこ

daughter

むすめ

autumn colors

もみじ

short

みじかい

ruler

ものさし

Hiragana Matching ひらがな マッチング

Connect the dots between each hiragana and the correct ro–maji.

に・	・mu
む・	・mi
も・	・nu
ぬ・	・ni
み・	・o
ま・	・mo
お・	・me
め・	・ma

Everyday Hiragana Words にちじょうの ことば

yo む
to read

のみもの
a drink

しつも n
question

なみだ
tears

うま
horse

あめ
candy

Answer Key こたえ あわせ

❑ Lesson 7: Word practice
1. も ri
3. む ri
5. みる
7. たべもの
9. のみもの
11. まほう

2. もみじ
4. めだつ
6. めがね
8. まも ru
10. むしあつい
12. みみず

❑ Lesson 7: Hiragana matching

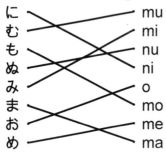

に — mu
む — mi
も — nu
ぬ — ni
み — o
ま — mo
お — me
め — ma

Lesson 8: Hiragana やゆよわをん

New Hiragana あたらしい ひらがな

Correct stroke order will mean neater characters when writing quickly.

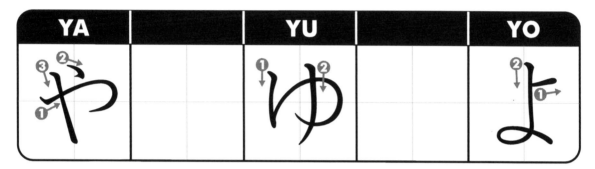

YA		YU		YO
や		ゆ		よ

WA		WO		N
わ		を		ん

Various Styles スタイル

Write each symbol as neatly as you can, then compare it to the different versions below.

や	や	や	や	や
ゆ	ゆ	ゆ	ゆ	ゆ
よ	よ	よ	よ	よ

わ	わ	わ	わ	わ
を	を	を	を	を
ん	ん	ん	ん	ん

Writing Practice れんしゅう

First trace the gray characters, then write each character six times.

ya	や	や					
yu	ゆ	ゆ					
yo	よ	よ					
wa	わ	わ					
wo	を	を					
n	ん	ん					

Word Practice ことばの れんしゅう

Fill in the appropriate hiragana in the blanks for each word.

1. ___ra う   (to laugh)
   wa

2. だいこ___   (radish)
   n

3. みず___のむ   (to drink water)
   wo

4. ___ru い   (bad)
   wa

5. ___たし   (me, I)
   wa

6. ほ___ ___かう   (buy a book)
   n   wo

7. こ___ ___   (tonight, this evening)
   n   ya

8. ___す reru   (to forget)
   wa

9. えいが ___み ru (to watch a movie)
   _{wo}

10. き___ぞく (metal)
    _n

11.か___た___ (easy)
    _n _n

12. すし___たべ ru (to eat sushi)
    _{wo}

Special Usage とくべつな つかいかた

❑ **The particle を (wo)**

The hiragana を is only used as a particle (object marker). It is never used for any other purpose. Even though "wo" is normally pronounced "o", お can never replace を as a particle.

> **Example Sentences**
> 1. てがみを (wo) かきます。   I will write a letter.
> 2. えんぴつを (wo) ください。 Give me a pencil please.

Words You Can Write かける ことば

Write the following words using the hiragana that you just learned.

alligator

わ	に								

roof

や	ね								

finger

ゆ	び								

garden

に	わ								

last night

ゆうべ

ring

ゆびわ

seaweed

わかめ

tonight

こんや

reservation, appointment

よやく

rumor

うわさ

(rice) paddy

たんぼ

surplus, composure

よゆう

easy

かんたん

human being

にんげん

Hiragana Matching ひらがな マッチング

Connect the dots between each hiragana and the correct ro–maji.

は・   ・yu

よ・   ・to

ゆ・   ・n

わ・   ・wo (o)

と・   ・ha

や・   ・wa

を・   ・yo

ん・   ・ya

Everyday Hiragana Words にちじょうの ことば

たいよう
the sun

うわぎ
jacket

ゆかた
light kimono

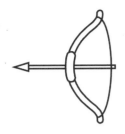

ゆみや

bow and arrow

かわかす

to dry

じてん sha

bicycle

Answer Key こたえ あわせ

❑ Lesson 8: Word practice

1. わ ra う
2. だいこん
3. みずを のむ
4. わ ru い
5. わたし
6. ほんを かう
7. こんや
8. わす reru
9. えいがを み ru
10. きんぞく
11. かんたん
12. すしを たべ ru

❑ Lesson 8: Hiragana matching

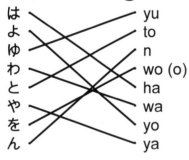

は　　　　yu
よ　　　　to
ゆ　　　　n
わ　　　　wo (o)
と　　　　ha
や　　　　wa
を　　　　yo
ん　　　　ya

Lesson 9: Hiragana らりるれろ

New Hiragana あたらしい ひらがな

Correct stroke order will mean neater characters when writing quickly.

RA	RI	RU	RE	

Various Styles スタイル

Write each symbol as neatly as you can, then compare it to the different versions below.

ら ら ら ら ら
り り り り り
る る る る る
れ れ れ れ れ
ろ ろ ろ ろ ろ

Writing Practice れんしゅう

First trace the gray characters, then write each character six times.

ra	ら	ら					
ri	り	り					
ru	る	る					
re	れ	れ					
ro	ろ	ろ					

Word Practice ことばの れんしゅう

Fill in the appropriate hiragana in the blanks for each word.

1. あた＿＿しい　(new)
   _{ra}

2. し＿＿　(to know)
   _{ru}

3. ＿＿んあい　(true love)
   _{re}

4. ＿＿んご　(apple)
   _{ri}

5. みせ＿＿　(to show)
   _{ru}

6. ＿＿ん shu う　(practice)
   _{re}

7. べん＿＿　(convenient)
   _{ri}

8. う＿＿おい　(moisture)
   _{ru}

9. かく＿＿んぼ　(hide and seek)
   _{re}

10. どう＿＿　(road)
    _{ro}

11. ＿＿うか　(hallway)
    _{ro}

12. まわ＿＿みち　(detour)
    _{ri}

Words You Can Write かける ことば

Write the following words using the hiragana that you just learned.

science

り	か										

night

よ	る										

impossible

む	り										

example

れ	い										

circle

ま	る										

monkey

さ	る										

ice

こ	お	り									

duck

あ	ひ	る									

camel

ら	く	だ									

frog, to return

| か | え | る | | | | | | | | | |

apple

| り | ん | ご | | | | | | | | | |

convenient

| べ | ん | り | | | | | | | | | |

left

| ひ | だ | り | | | | | | | | | |

management

| か | ん | り | | | | | | | | | |

yellow

| き | い | ろ | | | | | | | | | |

icicle

| つ | ら | ら | | | | | | | | | |

light blue

| み | ず | い | ろ | | | | | | |

candle

| ろ | う | そ | く | | | | | | |

forcibly

| む | り | や | り | | | | | | |

Hiragana Matching ひらがな マッチング

Connect the dots between each hiragana and the correct ro–maji.

る・	・ru
し・	・shi
り・	・re
ろ・	・i
ぬ・	・ro
れ・	・ra
い・	・nu
ら・	・ri

Everyday Hiragana Words にちじょうの ことば

ねる
to sleep, go to bed

いくら
salted salmon eggs

くすり
medicine

ろうそく

candle

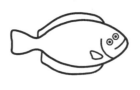

かれい

flounder

かみなり

thunder, lightning

Answer Key こたえ あわせ

❑ Lesson 9: Word practice

1. あたらしい
2. しる
3. れんあい
4. りんご
5. みせる
6. れん shu う
7. べんり
8. うるおい
9. かくれんぼ
10. どうろ
11. ろうか
12. まわりみち

❑ Lesson 9: Hiragana matching

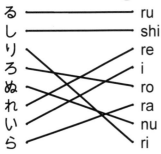

る ——————— ru
し ——————— shi
り ——————— re
ろ ——————— i
ぬ ——————— ro
れ ——————— ra
い ——————— nu
ら ——————— ri

Lesson 10: Compound Hiragana

New Hiragana あたらしい ひらがな

The final hiragana are easy! There are only 33 official hiragana left to learn - but don't let that number scare you. They are all made up of the hiragana that you already know. Just by looking at them you should already have an idea of the sound that they represent.

> **Examples**
>
> き (ki)   +   や (ya)   =   きゃ (kya)
>
> し (shi)   +   ゆ (yu)   =   しゅ (shu)
>
> ち (chi)   +   よ (yo)   =   ちょ (cho)

As you can see you add a small version of や、ゆ or よ to items in the い form of the hiragana.

Writing Points かくポイント

❏ **The correct way to write compound hiragana**

When writing compound hiragana, make sure that the second character is visibly smaller than the first character.

ro–maji	correct	incorrect
mya	みゃ	みや
ryo	りょ	りよ
chu	ちゅ	ちゆ
kya	きゃ	きや
pya	ぴゃ	ぴや

❑ Compound Hiragana

The following are the compound hiragana. They are created using the hiragana you already know so you should have no problem learning these.

きゃ kya	きゅ kyu	きょ kyo
ぎゃ gya	ぎゅ gyu	ぎょ gyo
しゃ sha	しゅ shu	しょ sho
じゃ ja	じゅ ju	じょ jo
ちゃ cha	ちゅ chu	ちょ cho
にゃ nya	にゅ nyu	にょ nyo

ひゃ hya	ひゅ hyu	ひょ hyo
びゃ bya	びゅ byu	びょ byo
ぴゃ pya	ぴゅ pyu	ぴょ pyo
みゃ mya	みゅ myu	みょ myo
りゃ rya	りゅ ryu	りょ ryo

Writing Practice れんしゅう

First trace the gray characters, then write each character six times.

KYA きゃ

KYU きゅ

KYO きょ

GYA ぎゃ

GYU ぎゅ

GYO ぎょ

SHA しゃ

SHU しゅ

SHO しょ

JA じゃ

JU じゅ

JO じょ

CHA ちゃ

CHU ちゅ

CHO ちょ

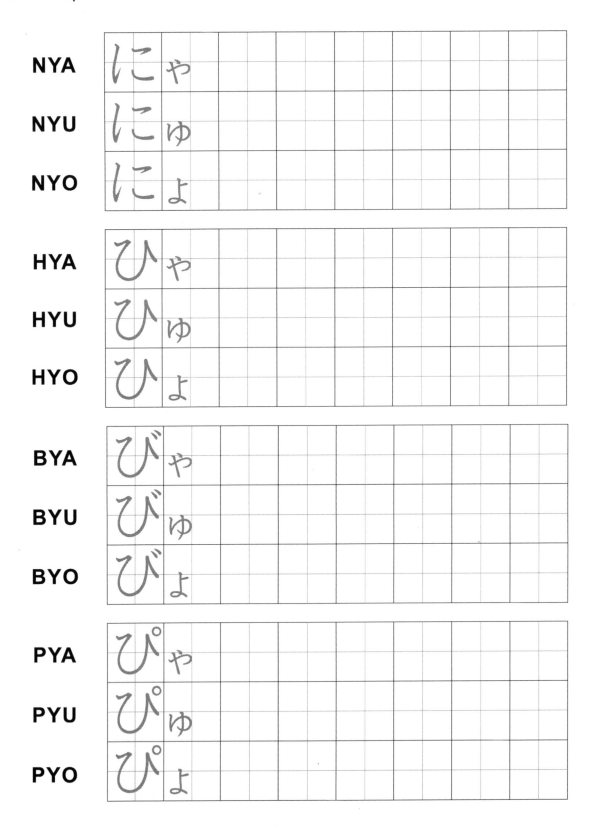

NYA にゃ

NYU にゅ

NYO にょ

HYA ひゃ

HYU ひゅ

HYO ひょ

BYA びゃ

BYU びゅ

BYO びょ

PYA ぴゃ

PYU ぴゅ

PYO ぴょ

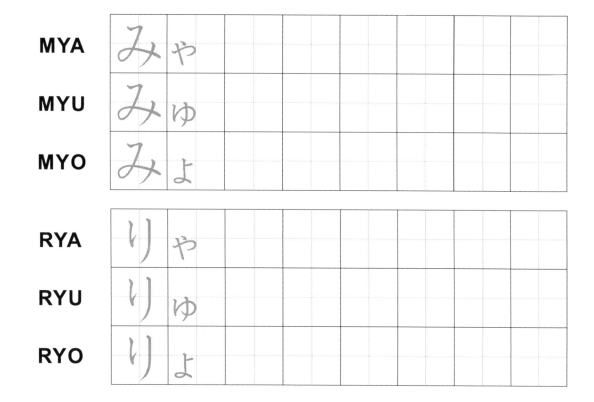

Word Practice ことばの れんしゅう

Fill in the appropriate hiragana in the blanks for each word.

1. とう___く   (arrival)
   <u>cha</u>

2. さん___く   (three hundred)
   <u>bya</u>

3. と___かん   (library)
   <u>sho</u>

4. ___う___う   (cow's milk)
   <u>gyu</u>   <u>nyu</u>

5. さん___く   (mountain range)
   <u>mya</u>

6. ___うばい   (business, commerce)
   <u>sho</u>

7. ___うたん   (carpet)
   <u>ju</u>

8. でん___う   (sales slip, voucher)
   <u>pyo</u>

9. ___うだい   (siblings)
   kyo

10. ___う___う   (dinosaur)
    kyo ryu

11. ___うがく   (study abroad)
    ryu

12. ___うどん   (beef bowl)
    gyu

Words You Can Write かける ことば

Write the following words using the compounds that you just learned.

butterfly

| ちょう | | | | | | | | | | | | |

nine (9)

| きゅう | | | | | | | | | | | | |

pulse

| みゃく | | | | | | | | | | | | |

dragon

| りゅう | | | | | | | | | | | | |

reverse

| ぎゃく | | | | | | | | | | | | |

song

| きょく | | | | | | | | | | | | |

capital city

| しゅと | | | | | | | | | | | | |

company

かいしゃ

sickness, sick

びょうき

veterinarian

じゅうい

Kyoto

きょうと

repair

しゅうり

travel

りょこう

train

でんしゃ

goldfish

きんぎょ

bowl

ちゃわん

investigation

ちょうさ

Hiragana Matching ひらがな マッチング

Connect the dots between each hiragana and the correct ro–maji.

ぎゃ・	・nyu
みょ・	・shu
しゅ・	・rya
ぴょ・	・ja
りゃ・	・myo
ちょ・	・pyo
じゃ・	・cho
にゅ・	・gya

Everyday Hiragana Words にちじょうの ことば

ちきゅうぎ
globe

しゅう
state

おちゃ
tea

べんきょう
study

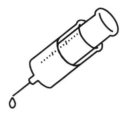

ちゅうしゃ
shot

しゅうり
repair

Answer Key こたえ あわせ

❑ Lesson 10: Word practice

1. とうちゃく
2. さんびゃく
3. としょかん
4. ぎゅうにゅう
5. さんみゃく
6. しょうばい
7. じゅうたん
8. でんぴょう
9. きょうだい
10. きょうりゅう
11. りゅうがく
12. ぎゅうどん

❑ Lesson 10: Hiragana matching

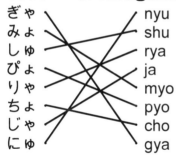

ぎゃ
みょ
しゅ
ぴょ
りゃ
ちょ
じゃ
にゅ

nyu
shu
rya
ja
myo
pyo
cho
gya

Hiragana Practice Sheet れんしゅう

Lesson 11: Katakana is next!

Congratulations on learning hiragana!
Here are some tips to help you reinforce what you have learned:

Let's put hiragana in our daily lives!

Write words on "post it" notes and then stick them on items. You can write しお and こしょう on your salt and pepper shakers using a permanent marker. This reinforces your skills even when you aren't thinking about it.

Read manga!

Some manga (Japanese comics) and children books have small hiragana next to the kanji. This is called "furigana". Look for furigana when purchasing manga. It's like Japanese on training wheels!

Keep on learning!

You have come this far, so keep up the momentum. Now let's learn katakana!

Why Learn Katakana?

New words are constantly being added to the Japanese language to cover new inventions such as smart phones, the internet, and new products etc. Many of these words are "borrowed" from other languages or even created by combining two words together. Words s not originally available in Japanese are written with katakana.

These words groups that are commonly written in katakana:
- foreign origin words   - foreign names
- country and city names   - product names
- company names   - plants and animals
- technical and scientific terms   - words for special emphasis
- onomatopoeia (words that imitate a sound)

❑ Lengthened sounds

   In katakana, the lengthening of vowel sounds is represented by a "yokobou", which means "horizontal line". When katakana is written from top to bottom, the line is referred to as "tatebou", which means "vertical line". Many Japanese people just simply call this lengthener "bou", which means "line". Any time you see a "bou" after one of the katakana characters, remember to lengthen the sound.

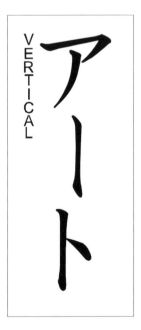

From this point we will immediately begin using this "bou" to lengthen sounds. Let's look at some common technology words that all contain lengthened sounds.

Example words
1. konpyu–ta–   computer
2. monita–   monitor
3. inta–netto   internet
4. heddofo–n   headphones
5. ki–bo–do   keyboard
6. suma–to fo–n   smart phone

❑ Long versus short sounds
With the borrowed words, called "gairaigo" in Japanese, the lengthened sound can change the meaning of the word.

> **Examples**
> kora   hey! (Japanese word)
> ko–ra–   cola (borrowed word)
>
> bin   bottle (Japanese word)
> bi–n   bean (borrowed word)
>
> pasu   path (borrowed word)
> pa–su   purse (borrowed word)

❑ Can I just say the borrowed words in English?
The short answer is "no". Even though many of the borrowed words come from English you will be better understood if you use the Japanese pronunciation. It is best to consider each of these words as Japanese words. For example, if you are a looking for a hotel in Japan, make sure you say *hoteru*. Also the original word for hotel in Japanese, りょかん, means "Japanese inn" which is a different style of hotel and maybe not what you are looking for.

The progressive system

From Zero! uses a PROGRESSIVE SYSTEM of teaching katakana. As you learn new katakana, we will immediately replace the Roman letters (ro-maji) with the katakana you have just learned. For example, after you learn オ (which sounds like "oh") we will mix it into the example words. To avoid confusion we won't mix in hiragana until after you have fully learned the katakana.

English	Before	After	After book
onion	onion	オ ni オ n	オニオン
owner	o–na–	オ—na—	オーナー

Lesson 12: Katakana アイウエオ

The goal ゴール

After the katakana lessons you will be able to read these characters.

46 standard katakana

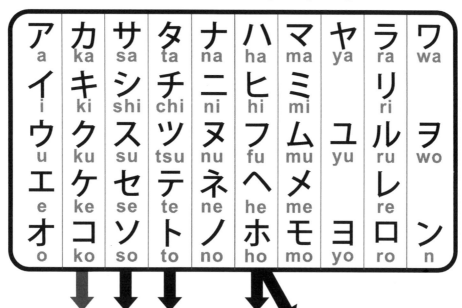

ア a	カ ka	サ sa	タ ta	ナ na	ハ ha	マ ma	ヤ ya	ラ ra	ワ wa
イ i	キ ki	シ shi	チ chi	ニ ni	ヒ hi	ミ mi		リ ri	
ウ u	ク ku	ス su	ツ tsu	ヌ nu	フ fu	ム mu	ユ yu	ル ru	ヲ wo
エ e	ケ ke	セ se	テ te	ネ ne	ヘ he	メ me		レ re	
オ o	コ ko	ソ so	ト to	ノ no	ホ ho	モ mo	ヨ yo	ロ ro	ン n

25 altered katakana

ガ ga	ザ za	ダ da	バ ba	パ pa
ギ gi	ジ ji	ヂ ji	ビ bi	ピ pi
グ gu	ズ zu	ヅ zu	ブ bu	プ pu
ゲ ge	ゼ ze	デ de	ベ be	ペ pe
ゴ go	ゾ zo	ド do	ボ bo	ポ po

Writing Basics かくときの きほん

❑ Different types of brush strokes

There are three types of strokes just like hiragana. Whether writing with a brush, pen, or pencil, make sure that you pay attention to the stroke type. This will ensure that your writing is neat and proper.

FADE OUT   DEAD STOP   BOUNCE FADE

The Japanese names for the strokes are as follows:

Fade out – harai (harau)
Dead stop – tome (tomeru)
Bounce fade – hane (haneru)

New Katakana あたらしい カタカナ

The first five katakana to learn are listed below. Notice the different stroke types. Be sure to learn the correct stroke order and stroke type.

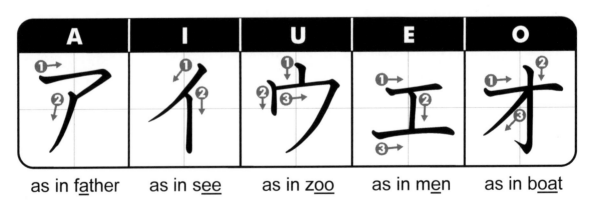

A	I	U	E	O
as in f<u>a</u>ther	as in s<u>ee</u>	as in z<u>oo</u>	as in m<u>e</u>n	as in b<u>oa</u>t

Various Styles スタイル

Write each symbol as neatly as you can, then compare it to the different versions below.

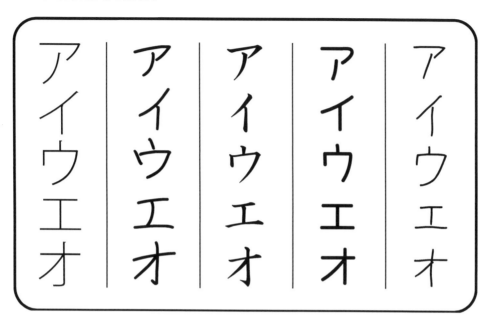

Writing Points かくポイント

❑ Continuous strokes

When writing ア and ウ you will notice that two of the strokes do not have stroke numbers. These are not independent strokes but instead a continuation of the prior stroke.

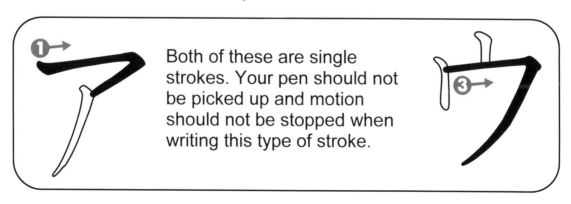

Both of these are single strokes. Your pen should not be picked up and motion should not be stopped when writing this type of stroke.

Writing Practice れんしゅう

First trace the gray characters, then write each character six times.

a	ア	ア					
i	イ	イ					
u	ウ	ウ					
e	エ	エ					
o	オ	オ					

Word Practice ことばの れんしゅう

In the Word Practice section of this book, you will fill in the appropriate katakana in the blanks for each word.

The roma–ji below the line tells you which katakana should be written. Notice the "bou" to show lengthened sounds are already included.

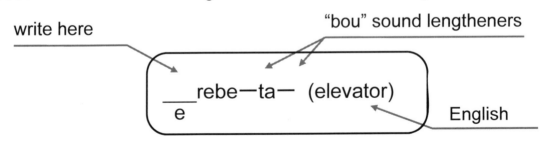

write here   "bou" sound lengtheners

___rebe－ta－ (elevator)
  e   English

1. ___rebe－ta－ (elevator)
   e

2. ___nime (animation)
   a

3. ___ ___kon (air conditioner)
   e   a

4. ___renji (orange)
   o

5. ___ba___to (sloppy, approximate)
　　a　　u

6. ___nku (ink)
　　i

7. ___tari___n (Italian)
　　i　　　a

8. ___muretsu (omelet)
　　o

9. ___—pun (open)
　　o

10. ___ ___nka— (car turn signal)
　　u　i

11. ___—mondo (almond)
　　a

12. ___ran (uranium)
　　u

Words You Can Write かける ことば

Write the following words using the katakana that you just learned.

letter "e"

イ	ー									

letter "a"

エ	イ									

letter "o"

オ	ー									

letter "i"

ア	イ									

French for "yes" (oui)

ウ	イ									

air

エ	ア	ー								

Katakana Matching カタカナ マッチング

Connect the dots between each katakana and the correct ro–maji.

エ・　　　　　・i

ア・　　　　　・u

オ・　　　　　・o

イ・　　　　　・a

ウ・　　　　　・e

Everyday Katakana Words にちじょうの ことば

ta オ ru
towel

ku イ zu
quiz

エ ー su
ace

オ ni オ n
onion

アイ su
ice cream

sa イ koro
dice

Answer Key こたえ あわせ

❑ Word Practice

1. エ rebe—ta—
2. ア nime
3. エア kon
4. オ renji
5. ア ba ウ to
6. イ nku
7. イ tari ア n
8. オ muretsu
9. オ—pun
10. ウイ nka—
11. ア—mondo
12. ウ ran

❑ Katakana Matching

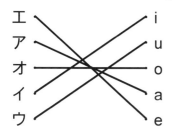

Katakana Practice Sheet れんしゅう

Lesson 13: Katakana カキクケコ

New Katakana あたらしい カタカナ

Correct stroke order will mean neater characters when writing quickly.

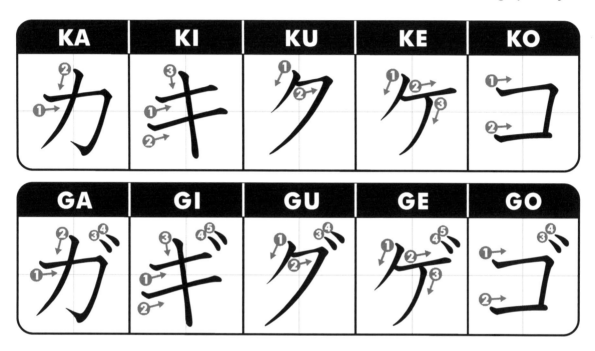

Various Styles スタイル

Write each symbol as neatly as you can, then compare it to the different versions below.

Writing Points かくポイント

❏ The dakuten

The only difference between *ka ki ku ke ko* and *ga gi gu ge go* are the last two small strokes up in the right hand corner. Those strokes are called *dakuten*.

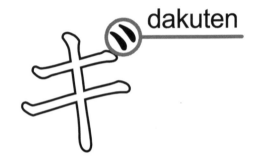

❏ Writing ク (ku) and ケ (ke) the correct way

Pay attention when writing ク and ケ as they can easily be written in a way that makes one look like the other.

Be careful not to extend the first stroke too far.

The second stroke is a continuous stroke.

KU

The third stroke should start from the middle of the second stroke.

KE

Writing Practice れんしゅう

First trace the gray characters, then write each character six times.

ka	カ	カ						
ki	キ	キ						
ku	ク	ク						
ke	ケ	ケ						
ko	コ	コ						

ga	ガ	ガ						
gi	ギ	ギ						
gu	グ	グ						
ge	ゲ	ゲ						
go	ゴ	ゴ						

Word Practice ことばの れんしゅう

Fill in the appropriate katakana in the blanks for each word.

1. ___ー___ru   (Google)
   gu   gu

2. ___mera   (camera)
   ka

3. ア furi___   (Africa)
   ka

4. ___ー hi ー   (coffee)
   ko

5. ___chappu   (ketchup)
   ke

6. ba イ rin___ru   (bilingual)
   ga

7. ___reyon   (crayon)
   ku

8. ___sorin   (gasoline)
   ga

9. bi___ni   (bikini)
   ki

10. ___ ___ba イ to   (gigabyte)
    gi   ga

11. イ ___risu   (England)
    gi

12. ___ー n   (corn)
    ko

Words You Can Write かける ことば

Write the following words using the katakana that you just learned.

key

キ	ー							

gear

ギ	ア							

core

コ	ア							

giga(byte)

ギ	ガ									

cake

ケ	ー	キ						

Coke

コ	ー	ク						

care

ケ	ア	ー						

cocoa

コ	コ	ア						

cargo

カ	ー	ゴ						

khaki

カ	ー	キ						

OK

オ	ー	ケ	ー						

squeak

キ	ー	キ	ー						

Katakana Matching カタカナ マッチング

Connect the dots between each katakana and the correct ro–maji.

ゲ・   ・ke

キ・   ・go

ク・   ・e

ゴ・   ・ki

エ・   ・ku

カ・   ・ge

ケ・   ・ka

Everyday Katakana Words にちじょうの ことば

カ－ten
curtain

su キ－
skiing

ta ク shi－
taxi

pan ケーキ
pancakes

taba コ
cigarettes,
tobacco

カ renda一
calendar

Answer Key こたえ あわせ

❏ Word Practice

1. グーグ ru
2. カ mera
3. ア furi カ
4. コーhi一
5. ケ chappu
6. ba イ rin ガ ru
7. ク reyon
8. ガ sorin
9. bi キ ni
10. ギガ ba イ to
11. イギ risu
12. コー n

❏ Katakana Matching

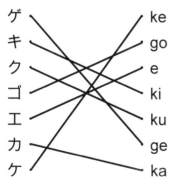

ゲ   ke
キ   go
ク   e
ゴ   ki
エ   ku
カ   ge
ケ   ka

Katakana Practice Sheet れんしゅう

Lesson 14: Katakana サシスセソ

New Katakana あたらしい カタカナ

Correct stroke order will mean neater characters when writing quickly.

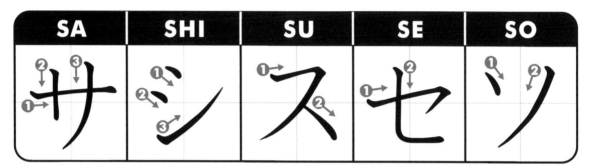

Various Styles スタイル

Write each symbol as neatly as you can, then compare it to the different versions below.

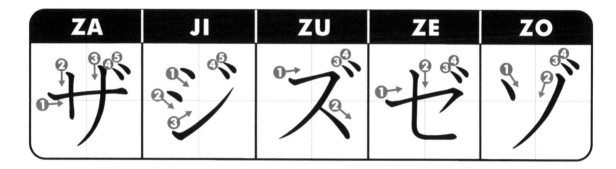

Writing Points かくポイント

❑ **Stroke order direction differences for シ (shi) and ソ (so)**
Though at first glance シ and ソ look a bit similar, the strokes for each character go in completely different directions.

A) The first 2 strokes for SHI are written with a slightly <u>horizontal</u> angle.

B) This stroke is written in an <u>upward</u> direction.

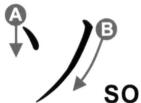

A) The first stroke for SO is written with a slightly <u>vertical</u> angle.

B) This stroke is written in a <u>downward</u> direction.

Writing Practice れんしゅう

First trace the gray characters, then write each character six times.

sa	サ	サ						
shi	シ	シ						
su	ス	ス						
se	セ	セ						
so	ソ	ソ						

za	ザ	ザ						
ji	ジ	ジ						
zu	ズ	ズ						
ze	ゼ	ゼ						
zo	ゾ	ゾ						

Word Practice ことばの れんしゅう

Fill in the appropriate katakana in the blanks for each word.

1. ___ーパー   (supermarket)
   su

2. ___futo   (software)
   so

3. ___nfuran___ ___コ (San Francisco)
   sa   shi   su

4. ___rada   (salad)
   sa

5. ___ーraー   (solar)
   so

6. ガー___   (guaze)
        ze

7. meron ___ーda   (melon soda)
          so

8. ___puーn   (spoon)
   su

9. ___ーtsu ケー___   (suitcase)
   su   su

10. ___ro   (zero)
    ze

11. ガ___rin   (gasoline)
       so

12. ___ーpan   (jeans)
    ji

Words You Can Write かける ことば

Write the following words using the katakana that you just learned.

kiss

キ	ス								

letter "C"

シ	ー								

gas

ガ	ス								

letter "S"

エ	ス								

ice

ア	イ	ス					

course

コ	ー	ス					

Switzerland

ス	イ	ス					

ski

ス	キ	ー					

quiz

ク	イ	ズ					

sauce

| ソ | ー | ス | | | | | | | | | |

Casio

| カ | シ | オ | | | | | | | | | |

Chicago

| シ | カ | ゴ | | | | | | | | | |

see-saw

| シ | ー | ソ | ー | | | | | | |

circus

| サ | ー | カ | ス | | | | | | |

zig zag

| ジ | グ | ザ | グ | | | | | | |

score

| ス | コ | ア | ー | | | | | | |

Caesar

| シ | ー | ザ | ー | | | | | | |

jigsaw puzzle

| ジ | グ | ソ | ー | | | | | | |

oasis

| オ | ア | シ | ス | | | | | | |

Katakana Matching カタカナ マッチング

Connect the dots between each katakana and the correct ro–maji.

ス・	・za
シ・	・ko
コ・	・se
エ・	・i
ザ・	・shi
ア・	・e
セ・	・su
イ・	・a

Everyday Katakana Words にちじょうの ことば

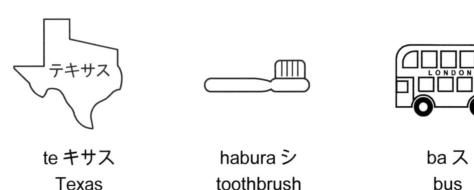

te キサス
Texas

habura シ
toothbrush

ba ス
bus

セーtaー
sweater

ガソ rin ス tando
gasoline station

ス toroー
straw

Answer Key こたえ あわせ

❏ Word Practice

1. スーpaー
2. ソ futo
3. サ nfuran シスコ
4. サ rada
5. ソーraー
6. ガーゼ
7. meron ソーda
8. ス puー n
9. スーツ ケース
10. ゼ ro
11. ガソ rin
12. ジーpan

❏ Katakana Matching

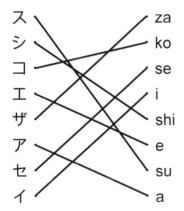

ス   za
シ   ko
コ   se
エ   i
ザ   shi
ア   e
セ   su
イ   a

Katakana Practice Sheet れんしゅう

Lesson 15: Katakana タチツテト

New Katakana あたらしい カタカナ

Correct stroke order will mean neater characters when writing quickly.

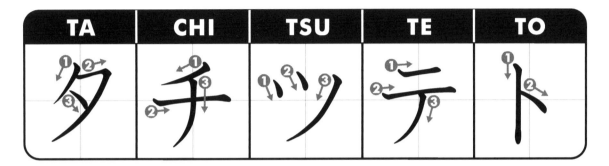

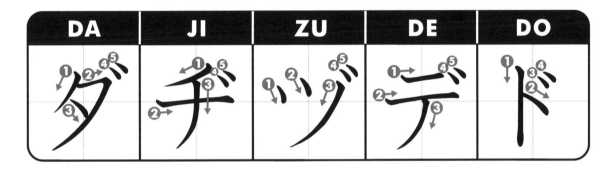

Various Styles スタイル

Write each symbol as neatly as you can, then compare it to the different versions below.

タ	タ	タ	タ	タ
チ	チ	チ	チ	チ
ツ	ツ	ツ	ツ	ツ
テ	テ	テ	テ	テ
ト	ト	ト	ト	ト

ダ	ダ	ダ	ダ	ダ
ヂ	ヂ	ヂ	ヂ	ヂ
ヅ	ヅ	ヅ	ヅ	ヅ
デ	デ	デ	デ	デ
ド	ド	ド	ド	ド

Writing Points かくポイント

❑ The double consonants

The double consonants (*kk, pp, tt, cch*) are stressed with a slight pause before the consonant. To represent them in katakana, a small ツ is used. The small ツ is always placed in front of the katakana that needs to be doubled.

Example		
bed	bed<u>do</u>	ベッド
McDonald's nick name	ma<u>kku</u>	マック
the letter "Z"	ze<u>tto</u>	ゼット

Make sure to write the ツ smaller than normal to avoid confusion with a normal ツ.

❑ The double consonant sound analysis

If you look at the sound wave for a word that has a double consonant, you will see a pause or visible space before the consonant. Look at the two samples below:

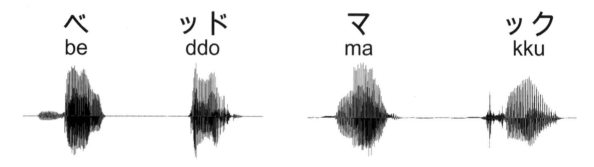

ベ	ッド	マ	ック
be	ddo	ma	kku

❑ Which version of *zu* and *ji* should be used?

There are two versions of *zu* and *ji*. The first set is in Lesson 3. ズ and ジ are more commonly used. ヅ and ヂ are used in only a few words, such as ヅラ (zura) (hairpiece) and チヂミ (chijimi) (a Korean pancake). Most dictionaries have less than 15 entries that contain ヅ or ヂ. If you're not sure about what version to use, try ズ and ジ and 90% of the time you will be correct.

❑ **The ツ sound**

To say ツ, (just like hiragana) start with the "TS" sound of "BOOTS" then add an ウ sound.

Writing Practice れんしゅう

First trace the gray characters, then write each character six times.

ta	タ	タ						
chi	チ	チ						
tsu	ツ	ツ						
te	テ	テ						
to	ト	ト						

da	ダ	ダ						
ji	ヂ	ヂ						
zu	ヅ	ヅ						
de	デ	デ						
do	ド	ド						

Word Practice ことばの れんしゅう

Fill in the appropriate katakana in the blanks for each word.

1. ___ス___ (test)
   te   to

2. ___ranpu (playing cards)
   to

3. ___ケッ___ (ticket)
   chi   to

4. ___npu (dump truck)
   da

5. コ npyu─___─ (computer)
   ta

6. ___ra ウ ma (trauma)
   to

7. ___イエッ___ (diet)
   da   to

8. ___─buru (table)
   te

9. イ n___─ne ッ___ (internet)
   ta   to

10. ___アー (tour)
    tsu

11. ___ジ___ru (digital)
    de   ta

12. ___ramu (drums)
    do

Words You Can Write かける ことば

Write the following words using the katakana that you just learned.

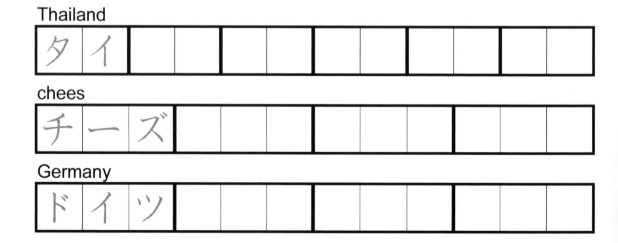

Thailand
タ イ

chees
チ ー ズ

Germany
ド イ ツ

date

デ	ー	ト									

card

カ	ー	ド									

soccer

サ	ッ	カ	ー								

cheetah

チ	ー	タ	ー								

taxi

タ	ク	シ	ー								

start

ス	タ	ー	ト								

steak

ス	テ	ー	キ								

cutter

カ	ッ	タ	ー								

skirt

ス	カ	ー	ト								

the sound of crying

シ	ク	シ	ク								

Katakana Matching カタカナ マッチング

Connect the dots between each katakana and the correct ro–maji.

サ・	・ji
ツ・	・da
テ・	・a
ア・	・chi
ダ・	・te
ジ・	・tsu
ス・	・sa
チ・	・su

Everyday Katakana Words にちじょうの ことば

サ n タ ク ro ー ス
Santa Claus

チケット
ticket

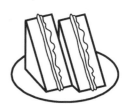

サ n ドイッチ
sandwich

po テト
french fries

ト ra ック
truck

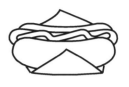

ho ットドッグ
hot dog

Answer Key こたえ あわせ

❑ Word Practice

1. テスト
2. ト ranpu
3. チケット
4. ダ npu
5. コ npyu ーター
6. ト ra ウ ma
7. ダイエット
8. テー buru
9. イ n ターネット
10. ツアー
11. デジタ ru
12. ド ramu

❑ Katakana Matching

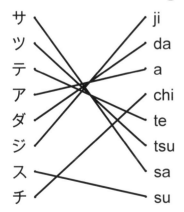

サ ── ji
ツ ── da
テ ── a
ア ── chi
ダ ── te
ジ ── tsu
ス ── sa
チ ── su

Katakana Practice Sheet れんしゅう

Lesson 16: Katakana ナニヌネノ

New Katakana あたらしい カタカナ

Correct stroke order will mean neater characters when writing quickly.

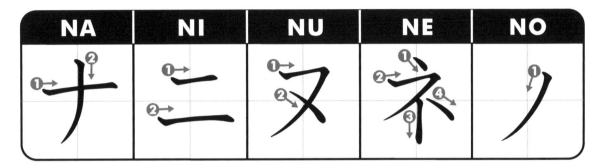

Various Styles スタイル

Write each symbol as neatly as you can, then compare it to the different versions below.

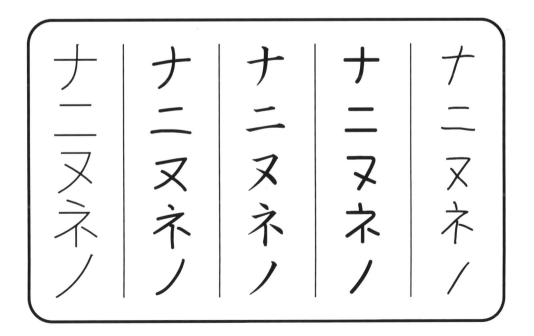

Writing Practice れんしゅう

First trace the gray characters, then write each character six times.

na	ナ	ナ					
ni	ニ	ニ					
nu	ヌ	ヌ					
ne	ネ	ネ					
no	ノ	ノ					

Word Practice ことばの れんしゅう

Fill in the appropriate katakana in the blanks for each word.

1. mi___raru (minerals)
   ne

2. ___イ―bu (naive)
   na

3. ___ー卜 pa ソコ n (laptop PC)
   no

4. ba___ra (vanilla)
   ni

5. ___ック___―mu (nick name)
   ni   ne

6. カ___ー (canoe)
   nu

7. ___ット wa―ク (network)
   ne

8. エコ___mi― (economy)
   no

9. カッ pu ___―ド ru (cup noodles)
   nu

10. ___pu キ n (napkin)
    na

11. mayo___―ズ (mayonaise)
    ne

12. mi___ban (mini-van)
    ni

Words You Can Write かける ことば

Write the following words using the katakana that you just learned.

no

ノ	ー								

tuna

ツ	ナ								

letter "N"

エ	ヌ								

node

ノ	ー	ド						

net

ネ	ッ	ト						

sauna

サ	ウ	ナ						

tennis

テ	ニ	ス						

knock

ノ	ッ	ク						

sonar

ソ	ナ	ー						

needs

ニ	ー	ズ								

noise

ノ	イ	ズ								

nude

ヌ	ー	ド								

nice

ナ	イ	ス								

NEET (young people not in education, employment or training)

ニ	ー	ト								

Ainu (indigenous people of northern Japan)

ア	イ	ヌ								

north

ノ	ー	ス								

necktie

ネ	ク	タ	イ						

night game

ナ	イ	タ	ー						

winding, meandering

ク	ネ	ク	ネ					

Katakana Matching カタカナ マッチング

Connect the dots between each katakana and the correct ro–maji.

ネ・   ・sa

タ・   ・tsu

ツ・   ・ta

ナ・   ・na

ヌ・   ・ni

サ・   ・ne

ニ・   ・nu

ノ・   ・no

Everyday Katakana Words にちじょうの ことば

ノート
notebook

mayo ネーズ
mayonnaise

ノ mi
flea

bi ジネス
business

ナ bi
navigation

SONY.

ソニー
Sony

Answer Key こたえ あわせ

❑ Word Practice

1. mi ネ raru
2. ナイーbu
3. ノート pa ソコ n
4. ba 二 ra
5. ニックネーmu
6. カヌー
7. ネット waーク
8. エコノ miー
9. カッ pu ヌード ru
10. ナ pu キ n
11. mayo ネーズ
12. mi 二 ban

❑ Katakana Matching

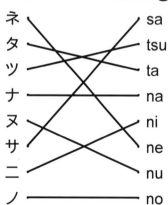

ネ	sa
タ	tsu
ツ	ta
ナ	na
ヌ	ni
サ	ne
二	nu
ノ	no

Lesson 17: Katakana ハヒフヘホ

New Katakana あたらしい カタカナ

Correct stroke order will mean neater characters when writing quickly.

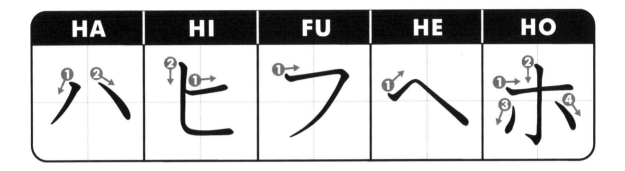

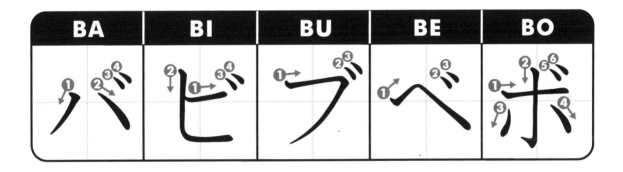

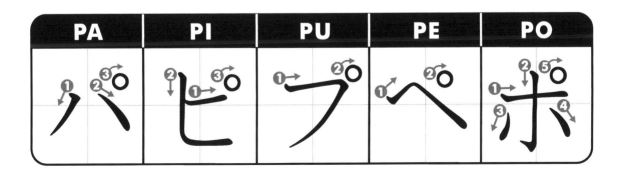

Various Styles スタイル

Write each symbol as neatly as you can, then compare it to the different versions below.

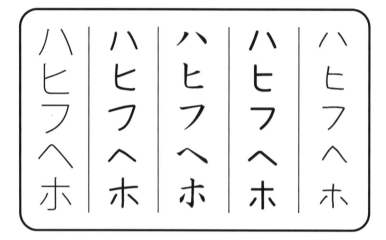

ハ ヒ フ ヘ ホ

バ ビ ブ ベ ボ

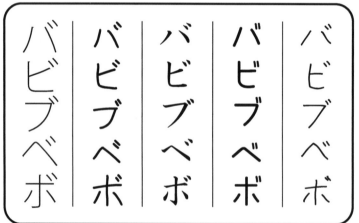

パ ピ プ ペ ポ

Writing Points かくポイント

❑ **What is that circle?**

The *pa pi pu pe po* katakana are made by adding a circle in the area where *dakuten* normally go. The circle is written clockwise and is always the last stroke. Most Japanese people refer to this as simply *maru*, which means "circle." The official name for it is *handakuten*.

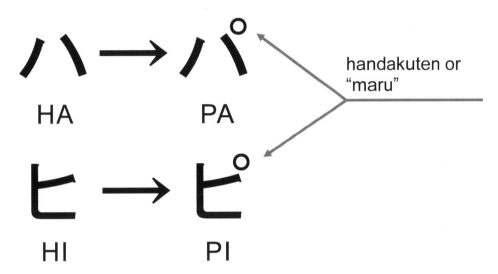

ハ → パ

HA   PA

handakuten or "maru"

ヒ → ピ

HI   PI

Writing Practice れんしゅう

First trace the gray characters, then write each character six times.

ha	ハ	ハ					
hi	ヒ	ヒ					
fu	フ	フ					
he	ヘ	ヘ					
ho	ホ	ホ					

ba	バ	バ						
bi	ビ	ビ						
bu	ブ	ブ						
be	ベ	ベ						
bo	ボ	ボ						

pa	パ	パ						
pi	ピ	ピ						
pu	プ	プ						
pe	ペ	ペ						
po	ポ	ポ						

Word Practice ことばの れんしゅう

Fill in the appropriate katakana in the blanks for each word.

1. ___rin ター   (printer)
   pu

2. ___n ク   (flat tire)
   pa

3. ___ーター (heater)
   hi

4. ___ru (bell)
   be

5. ___ーru___n (ball pen)
   bo   pe

6. ___タ min (vitamin)
   bi

7. ___ッチキス (stapler)
   ho

8. ___アス (pierced earrings)
   pi

9. ___ーmu___ージ (home page)
   ho   pe

10. ya___ー (Yahoo!)
    fu

11. ___イキnグ (all you can eat buffet)
    ba

12. ___nチ (bench)
    be

Words You Can Write かける ことば

Write the following words using the katakana that you just learned.

papa

パ	パ							

letter "P"

ピ	ー							

bus

バ	ス							

mail box

ポ	ス	ト					

beach

ビ	ー	チ					

cup

コップ

page

ページ

jeep

ジープ

butter

バター

soup

スープ

boat

ボート

tape

テープ

pocket

ポケット

peanuts

ピーナツ

poster

ポスター

Katakana Matching カタカナ マッチング

Connect the dots between each katakana and the correct ro–maji.

フ ·	· pi
ハ ·	· pe
ザ ·	· ha
ボ ·	· fu
ペ ·	· gu
デ ·	· za
ピ ·	· de
グ ·	· bo

Everyday Katakana Words にちじょうの ことば

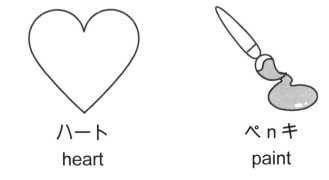

ハート
heart

ペnキ
paint

ポップコーn
popcorn

ピザ
pizza

ゴ ru フ
golf

ハ n バーガー
hamburger

Answer Key こたえ あわせ

❏ Word Practice

1. プ rin ター
2. パ n ク
3. ヒーター
4. べ ru
5. ボー ru ペ n
6. ビタ min
7. ホッチキス
8. ピアス
9. ホー mu ページ
10. ya フー
11. バイキ n グ
12. べ n チ

❏ Katakana Matching

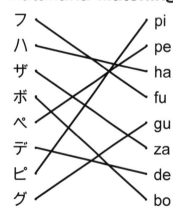

フ	pi
ハ	pe
ザ	ha
ボ	fu
ペ	gu
デ	za
ピ	de
グ	bo

Lesson 18: Katakana マミムメモ

New Katakana あたらしい カタカナ

Correct stroke order will mean neater characters when writing quickly.

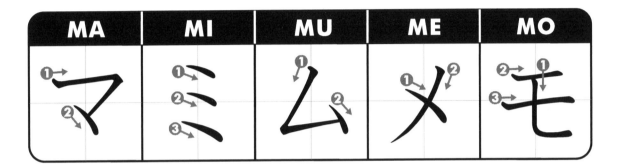

Various Styles スタイル

Write each symbol as neatly as you can, then compare it to the different versions below.

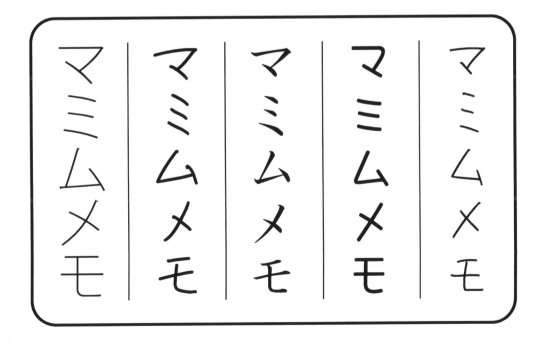

Writing Points かくポイント

❑ **The difference between ア (a) and マ (ma)**

Be sure when writing マ that you don't unintentionally draw an ア.

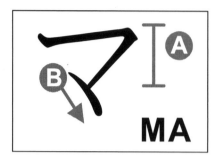
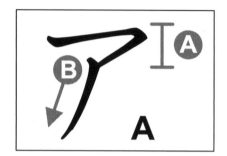

A) The height of the top portion of マ (MA) takes up more than half of the entire height of the character, while the top of ア (A) takes up less than half.

B) The angles of this stroke are different for each character. The type of strokes are also different; マ (MA) is a dead stop and ア (A) is a fade out.

Writing Practice れんしゅう

First trace the gray characters, then write each character six times.

ma	マ	マ					
mi	ミ	ミ					
mu	ム	ム					
me	メ	メ					
mo	モ	モ					

Word Practice ことばの れんしゅう

Fill in the appropriate katakana in the blanks for each word.

1. ___ーru アド re ス (mail address)

me

2. ___イク (make-up)

me

3. ___ーター (motor)

mo

4. ___n ガ (manga, comics)

ma

5. ハ___サ n ド (ham sandwich)

mu

6. ___サイ ru (missile)

mi

7. ___ット re ス (mattress)

ma

8. ナト ri ウ___ (sodium)

mu

9. ア ru ___ (aluminum)

mi
mode)

10. ___ナー___ード (silent

ma   mo

11. ___ーru (shopping mall)

mo

12. ___n バー (member)

me

Words You Can Write かける ことば

Write the following words using the katakana that you just learned.

letter "M"

エ	ム								

ham

ハ	ム								

memo

メ	モ								

mini

ミ	ニ									

peach

モ	モ									

Nemo (the fish)

ニ	モ									

match

マ	ッ	チ							

game

ゲ	ー	ム							

theme

テ	ー	マ							

mask

マ	ス	ク							

mass communication (the media)

マ	ス	コ	ミ					

monitor

モ	ニ	タ	ー					

slim, stylish

ス	マ	ー	ト					

Katakana Matching カタカナ マッチング

Connect the dots between each katakana and the correct ro–maji.

ヌ ・	・ mu
モ ・	・ mi
メ ・	・ nu
ニ ・	・ ma
ミ ・	・ o
マ ・	・ mo
オ ・	・ me
ム ・	・ ni

Everyday Katakana Words にちじょうの ことば

マクドナ ru ド
McDonald's

ミミズ
earthworm

ガム
gum

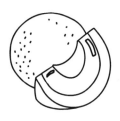

メ ron

melon

モバイ ru

mobile

ママ

mama

Answer Key こたえ あわせ

❑ Word Practice

1. メーru アド re ス
2. メイク
3. モーター
4. マ n ガ
5. ハムサ n ド
6. ミサイ ru
7. マット re ス
8. ナト ri ウ mu
9. ア ru ミ
10. マナーモード
11. モー ru
12. メ n バー

❑ Katakana Matching

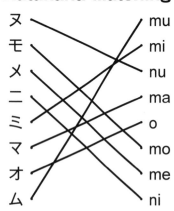

ヌ — mu
モ — mi
メ — nu
ニ — ma
ミ — o
マ — mo
オ — me
ム — ni

Lesson 19: Katakana ヤユヨワヲン

New Katakana あたらしい カタカナ

Correct stroke order will mean neater characters when writing quickly.

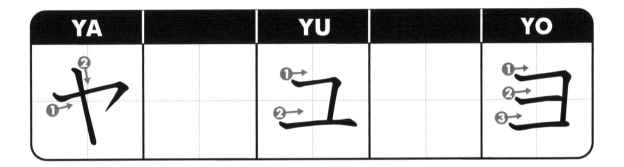

Various Styles スタイル

Write each symbol as neatly as you can, then compare it to the different versions below.

ヤ	ヤ	ヤ	ヤ	ヤ
ユ	ユ	ユ	ユ	ユ
ヨ	ヨ	ヨ	ヨ	ヨ

ワ	ワ	ワ	ワ	ワ
ヲ	ヲ	ヲ	ヲ	ヲ
ン	ン	ン	ン	ン

Writing Points かくポイント

❏ **The difference between ユ (yu) and コ (ko)**
When writing ユ (yu) that you don't unintentionally draw コ (ko).

YU  Make sure the second stroke extends past the first stroke.

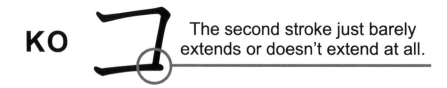

KO ﾕ The second stroke just barely extends or doesn't extend at all.

Writing Practice れんしゅう

First trace the gray characters, then write each character six times.

ya	ヤ	ヤ						
yu	ユ	ユ						
yo	ヨ	ヨ						
wa	ワ	ワ						
wo	ヲ	ヲ						
n	ン	ン						

Word Practice ことばの れんしゅう

Fill in the appropriate katakana in the blanks for each word.

1. ド ra イ___ー (hair dryer)

ya

2. デザイ___ (design)

n

3. ___ーro ッパ (Europe)

yo

4. ___ニバーサ ru (universal)

yu

5. タイ___ (tire)

ya

6. ___ーザー (user)

yu

7. ___クチ___ (vaccine)

wa   n

8. ___ーモア (humour)

yu

9. フ ri―ダイ___ru (toll free number)

ya

10. ___イ n (wine)

wa

11. ___ーグ ru ト (yogurt)

yo

12. ___タ (nerd, geek)

wo

Special Usage とくべつな つかいかた

❑ **The particle ヲ (wo)**
The katakana ヲ is rarely used. One of the only words where you MIGHT see it used is ヲタ (short for ヲタク which means "nerd or geek"). Even this word is often spelled as オタク.

In the rare case that you are playing Zelda or another game on an old "Family Computer" (Famicon – Japan's name for the first popular Nintendo game system) or even a Japanese game boy, you might see this used as a particle (object marker). Even though "wo" can also be pronounced "o", オ can never replace ヲ as a particle.

Words You Can Write かける ことば

Write the following words using the katakana that you just learned.

bread

パ	ン								

letter "Y"

ワ	イ								

Utah (state)

ユ	タ								

tower

タ	ワ	ー							

yacht

ヨ	ッ	ト							

combination

コ	ン	ビ							

signature

サ	イ	ン							

coin

コ	イ	ン							

tale, short play

コ	ン	ト							

wasp

ワ	ス	プ									

otaku

ヲ	タ	ク									

youth

ユ	ー	ス									

one man (a bus operated without a tour guide)

ワ	ン	マ	ン						

yo-yo

ヨ	ー	ヨ	ー						

bacon

ベ	ー	コ	ン						

won ton (soup)

ワ	ン	タ	ン						

bow-wow

ワ	ン	ワ	ン						

hammer

ハ	ン	マ	ー						

the sound of being excited

ワ	ク	ワ	ク						

Katakana Matching カタカナ マッチング

Connect the dots between each katakana and the correct ro–maji.

ツ ·   · yu

テ ·   · te

ユ ·   · tsu

シ ·   · so

ヨ ·   · ha

ヤ ·   · shi

ソ ·   · yo

ハ ·   · ya

Everyday Katakana Words にちじょうの ことば

ヨガ
yoga

ユ ri
lily

タイワン
Taiwan

ワシントン
Washington

ダイヤモンド
diamond

ヤギ
goat

Answer Key こたえ あわせ

❏ Word Practice

1. ド ra イヤー
2. デザイン
3. ヨーro ッパ
4. ユニバーサ ru
5. タイヤ
6. ユーザ
7. ワクチン
8. ユーモア
9. フ ri ーダイヤ ru
10. ワイン
11. ヨーグ ru ト
12. ヲタ

❏ Katakana Matching

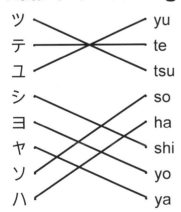

ツ yu
テ te
ユ tsu
シ so
ヨ ha
ヤ shi
ソ yo
ハ ya

Katakana Practice Sheet れんしゅう

Lesson 20: Katakana ラリルレロ

New Katakana あたらしい カタカナ

Correct stroke order will mean neater characters when writing quickly.

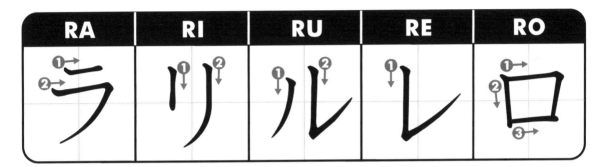

RA	RI	RU	RE	RO

Various Styles スタイル

Write each symbol as neatly as you can, then compare it to the different versions below.

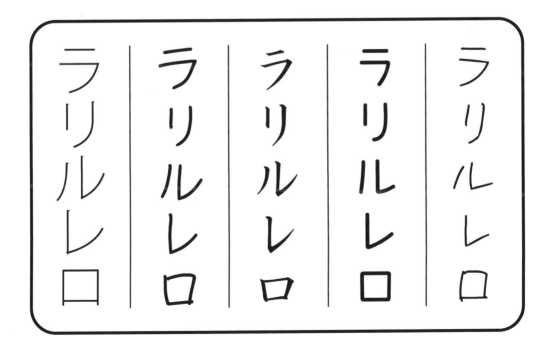

Writing Practice れんしゅう

First trace the gray characters, then write each character six times.

ra	ラ	ラ						
ri	リ	リ						
ru	ル	ル						
re	レ	レ						
ro	ロ	ロ						

Word Practice ことばの れんしゅう

Fill in the appropriate katakana in the blanks for each word.

1. ___ストラン (restaurant)
   re

2. タオ___ (towel)
   ru

3. ___ーメン (raamen noodles)
   ra

4. バ___ー (volley ball)
   re

5. ウー___ (wool)
   ru

6. モノ___ー___ (monorail)
   re   ru

7. ヘ___メット (helmet)
   ru

8. ___ープ (rope)
   ro

9. バ＿＿ンス (balance)

ra

10. インテ＿＿＿ (intelligence)

ri

11. ＿＿シア (Russia)

ro

12. アイド＿＿＿ (idol)

ru

Words You Can Write かける ことば

Write the following words using the katakana that you just learned.

ruby

ル	ビ								

ribbon

リ	ボ	ン						

ball

ボ	ー	ル						

lettuce

レ	タ	ス						

real

リ	ア	ル						

rare

レ	ア	ー						

lock, rock (music)

ロ	ッ	ク						

letter "r"

アール

rally

ラリー

roll

ロール

robot

ロボット

lesson

レッスン

fruit

フルーツ

remote control

リモコン

rocket

ロケット

lion

ライオン

repeat

リピート

Katakana Matching カタカナ マッチング

Connect the dots between each katakana and the correct ro–maji.

ル・	・chi
レ・	・mi
リ・	・ra
イ・	・re
チ・	・ro
ミ・	・i
ロ・	・ru
ラ・	・ri

Everyday Katakana Words にちじょうの ことば

サングラス
sunglasses

セロテープ
cellophane tape

ソフトクリーム
soft serve ice cream

リモコン
remote control

クレジットカード
credit card

ランプ
lamp

Answer Key こたえ あわせ

❏ Word Practice

1. レストラン
2. タオル
3. ラーメン
4. バレー
5. ウール
6. モノレール
7. ヘルメット
8. ロープ
9. バランス
10. インテリ
11. ロシア
12. アイドル

❏ Katakana Matching

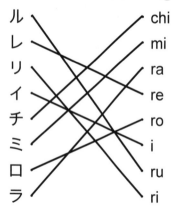

ル   chi
レ   mi
リ   ra
イ   re
チ   ro
ミ   i
ロ   ru
ラ   ri

Lesson 21: Compound Katakana

The final katakana are easy! There are only 33 official katakana left to learn - but don't let that number scare you. They are all made up of the katakana that you already know. Just by looking at them you should already have an idea of the sound that they represent.

Examples

キ (ki)	+	ヤ (ya)	=	キャ (kya)
シ (shi)	+	ユ (yu)	=	シュ (shu)
チ (chi)	+	ヨ (yo)	=	チョ (cho)

Writing Points かくポイント

❑ **The correct way to write compound katakana**
When writing compound katakana, make sure that the second character is visibly smaller than the first character.

ro-maji	correct	incorrect
mya	ミャ	ミヤ
ryo	リョ	リヨ
chu	チュ	チユ
kya	キャ	キヤ
pya	ピャ	ピヤ

❑ **Katakana word separation**
When there are two or more katakana words in succession, a small dot is sometimes placed between them to separate the words.
This is so it is easier to tell when one word ends and another starts.
When you write your name you can put a dot between your first and last name to show clearly separate them. This dot is not required, but it really helps readability.

Examples

ジョン・スミス (John Smith)
ケース・バイ・ケース (case by case)
ジョージ・ワシントン (George Washington)

❑ Compound katakana

The following are compound katakana.

キャ kya	キュ kyu	キョ kyo
ギャ gya	ギュ gyu	ギョ gyo
シャ sha	シュ shu	ショ sho
ジャ ja	ジュ ju	ジョ jo
チャ cha	チュ chu	チョ cho
ニャ nya	ニュ nyu	ニョ nyo

ヒャ hya	ヒュ hyu	ヒョ hyo
ビャ bya	ビュ byu	ビョ byo
ピャ pya	ピュ pyu	ピョ pyo
ミャ mya	ミュ myu	ミョ myo
リャ rya	リュ ryu	リョ ryo

Writing Practice れんしゅう

First trace the gray characters, then write each character six times.

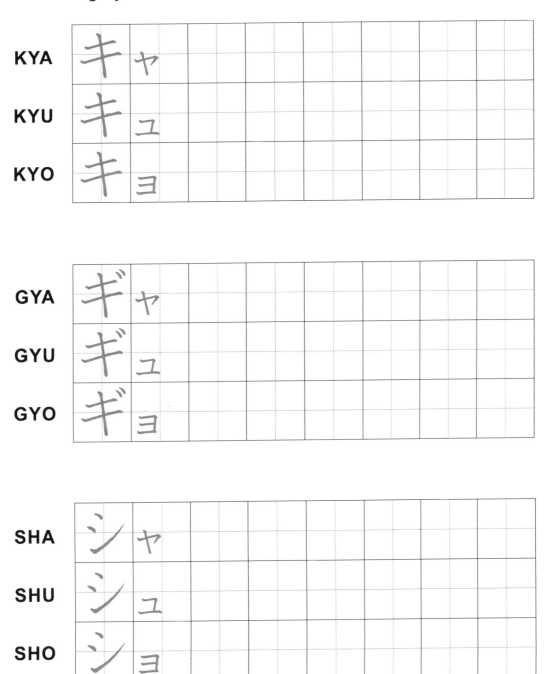

JA ジャ

JU ジュ

JO ジョ

CHA チャ

CHU チュ

CHO チョ

NYA ニャ

NYU ニュ

NYO ニョ

HYA ヒャ

HYU ヒュ

HYO ヒョ

BYA	ビャ							
BYU	ビュ							
BYO	ビョ							

PYA	ピャ							
PYU	ピュ							
PYO	ピョ							

MYA	ミャ							
MYU	ミュ							
MYO	ミョ							

RYA	リャ							
RYU	リュ							
RYO	リョ							

Word Practice ことばの れんしゅう

Fill in the appropriate katakana in the blanks for each word.

1. メッ＿＿＿ (mesh)
   shu

2. マニ＿＿＿ア (manicure)
   kyu

3. ＿＿＿ックサック (back pack)
   ryu

4. バー＿＿＿ン (version)
   jo

5. ＿＿＿レンジ (challenge)
   cha

6. ＿＿＿ーヨーク (New York)
   nyu

7. ＿＿＿コレート (chocolate)
   cho

8. ナ＿＿＿ラル (natural)
   chu

9. ＿＿＿ンブル (gamble)
   gya

10. ＿＿＿ラメル (caramel)
    kya

11. ＿＿＿ーマン (human)
    hyu

12. ＿＿＿ーリップ (tulip)
    chu

Words You Can Write かける ことば

Write the following words using the katakana that you just learned.

pure

ピ	ュ	ア									

letter "H"

エ	ッ	チ									

cabbage

キ	ャ	ベ	ツ							

juice

ジュース

choice

チョイス

caviar

キャビア

joke

ジョーク

menu

メニュー

chance

チャンス

shower

シャワー

jump

ジャンプ

backpack

リュック

fuse

ヒュース

Katakana Matching カタカナ マッチング

Connect the dots between each katakana and the correct ro–maji.

ギャ ·	· ja
ニュ ·	· cho
ジャ ·	· rya
ピョ ·	· nyu
リャ ·	· pyo
チョ ·	· myu
ミュ ·	· ju
ジュ ·	· gya

Everyday Katakana Words にちじょうの ことば

ジュース
juice

ニュース
news

コンピューター
computer

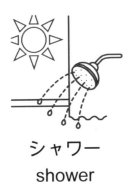

シャワー
shower

ジャケット
jacket

インターナショナル
international

Answer Key こたえ あわせ

❏ Word Practice

1. メッシュ
2. マニキュア
3. リュックサック
4. バージョン
5. チャレンジ
6. ニューヨーク
7. チョコレート
8. ナチュラル
9. ギャンブル
10. キャラメル
11. ヒューマン
12. チューリップ

❏ Katakana Matching

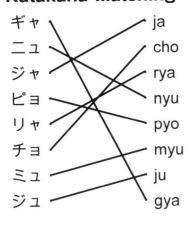

ギャ	ja
ニュ	cho
ジャ	rya
ピョ	nyu
リャ	pyo
チョ	myu
ミュ	ju
ジュ	gya

Katakana Practice Sheet れんしゅう

Lesson 22: Unique Compounds

Katakana is unique because it represents words that are foreign origin. Because of this, there are some combinations that are normally not used in hiragana.

Here are some of the possible combinations.

Katakana	Romanization	Sounds Like
ティ	ti	letter "T"
ディ	di	letter "D"
チェ	che	check
トゥ	tu	two
ドゥ	du	do
シェ	she	shed
ジェ	je	jeff
ヴァ	va	<u>va</u>rnish
ウィ	wi	week
ウェ	we	wet
ウォ	wo	woah
ファ	fa	<u>fa</u>ther
フィ	fi	feet
フェ	fe	feather
フォ	fo	phone

Word Practice ことばの れんしゅう

Fill in the appropriate katakana in the blanks for each word.

1. ＿＿ットコースター (roller coaster)
   je

2. ブルー＿＿＿ス (Bluetooth)
   tu

3. ＿＿リピン (Philippines)
   fi

4. パー＿＿クト (perfect)
   fe

5. ＿＿イク (shake)
   she

6. ネグリ＿＿＿ (neglige)
   je

7. ＿＿キピ＿＿ア (Wikipedia)
   wi   di

8. ソフト＿＿アー (software)
   we

9. ＿＿イアー＿＿ール (firewall)
   fa   wo

10. ＿＿ラシー (jealousy)
    je

11. ＿＿ミレス (family restaurant)
    fa

12. ＿＿スカウント (discount)
    di

Words You Can Write かける ことば

Write the following words using the katakana that you just learned.

tea

ティー							

letter "J"

ジェー							

web (world wide web)

ウェブ							

cello

チェロ

Wii (Nintendo)

ウィー

Jane

ジェーン

sofa

ソファー

fork

フォーク

today

トゥデイ

Norway

ノルウェー

tissue

ティッシュ

CD (compact disc)

シーディー

shaver

シェイバー

Katakana Matching カタカナ マッチング

Connect the dots between each katakana and the correct ro–maji.

チェ・　　　　・va

シェ・　　　　・fo

フォ・　　　　・tu

フィ・　　　　・che

ウェ・　　　　・she

ヴァ・　　　　・fi

ディ・　　　　・di

トゥ・　　　　・we

Everyday Katakana Words にちじょうの ことば

キャンディー
candy

ウェルダン
well done (cooking)

ティー
tea

ファッション
fashion

フィールド
field

ジェット
jet

Answer Key こたえ あわせ

❑ Word Practice

1. ジェットコースター
2. ブルートゥース
3. フィリピン
4. パーフェクト
5. シェイク
6. ネグリジェ
7. ウィキピディア
8. ソフトウェー
9. ファイアーワォール
10. ジェラシー
11. ファミレス
12. ディスカウント

❑ Katakana Matching

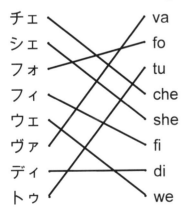

チェ	va
シェ	fo
フォ	tu
フィ	che
ウェ	she
ヴァ	fi
ディ	di
トゥ	we

Katakana Practice Sheet れんしゅう

Lesson 23: The Next Step

Congratulations on learning katakana
Here are some tips to help you reinforce what you have learned:

Let's put katakana in our daily lives!
Write words in katakana on "post it" notes and then stick them on items around your house. You can even write ソルト and ペッパー on your salt and pepper shakers using a permanent marker. This will enforce your skills even when you aren't thinking about it.

Look for katakana everywhere!

Every Japanese newspaper, magazine, and website uses a LOT of katakana. Look and see how many of the katakana words you can decipher! You will be surprised how many "Japanese" words you now know that you can read katakana!

Keep on learning!

Your next step is to begin learning kanji! You have come this far, so keep up the momentum. As a bonus to this book the first two lessons from "**Kanji From Zero!**" book 1 is included after this. Kanji is the key to truly grasping Japanese.

George and Yukari Trombley – JapaneseFromZero.com

After learning the kana Japanese begin learning the 2000+ kanji characters. Continue learning with the "*Kanji From Zero!*" series.

As a special bonus and in hopes that you will continue learning with our books we have included the first 2 lessons from
Kanji From Zero! book 1.

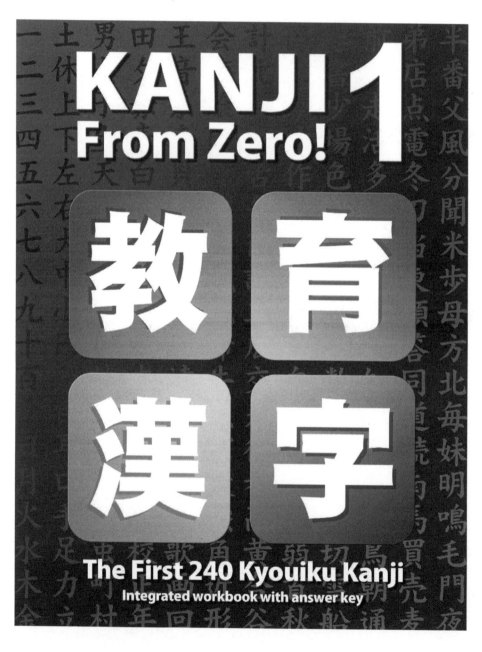

Lesson 24: Kanji Basics

Kanji Basics かんじの きほん

❑ Why kanji are important

Welcome to kanji, and congratulations for coming this far in your quest to learn Japanese. Many students ask, "Is it really necessary to learn the kanji?" The answer is *yes*. The kanji are not just phonetic symbols like hiragana and katakana. Each kanji has meaning. By learning the kanji you will be able to make sense of how words are related to each other, and your ability to understand Japanese will increase substantially as you learn new characters.

The kanji 食 can be read as しょく or た, depending on the word. The kanji 食 means "food," and words with this kanji in them tend to have meanings related to food. Even if you didn't know the word, you would know that it is related to food if this kanji were in it. Consider the following words that use this kanji:

食堂 しょくどう　　cafeteria
食卓 しょくたく　　dinner table
食欲 しょくよく　　appetite
食品 しょくひん　　food products
夕食 ゆうしょく　　dinner
食中毒　しょくちゅうどく　food poisoning
夜食 やしょく　midnight snack

As you can see, all of the words have 食 in them and are somehow related to food.

❑ Listening for kanji

Kanji are great because they give you a level of comprehension not available from hiragana and katakana alone. For example, if you hear the word にほんしょく, even though you have never heard the word before you might be able to understand what it means based on the kanji you have "heard." Because you know that にほん

means Japan, and you know that しょく is one of the readings for the kanji "food," you could assume that the word means "Japanese food." Of course, it is possible that the しょく portion of にほんしょく was not the kanji for food but the kanji for color, 色, which can also be read as しょく. You can rule out other kanji possibilities by the context of the conversation.

Knowing how words are written in kanji helps comprehension because you can guess what something means based on what the possible kanji are. Learning kanji is not as easy as learning hiragana or katakana, but the benefits of knowing kanji make it worthwhile.

❑ Different readings

Unlike hiragana and katakana, kanji can have more than one reading. The best way to learn the different readings is to learn a word that uses the particular reading. The kanji section of the lesson will provide you with sample words for each reading.

There are two types of readings:
くんよみ is the Japanese reading of the kanji. It is normally unique to the Japanese language.

おんよみ is the Chinese reading of the kanji. If you ever study Chinese, you will notice the similarity in the way the kanji is read in both languages. Sometimes the おんよみ of the kanji sounds *nothing* like it does in Chinese.

❑ Reading instinct

Many students struggle with kanji because they are not sure whether the kanji in the word should be read with the おんよみ or くんよみ. Although there is no foolproof way to know which reading to use, you will usually be correct if you follow this simple guideline: most kanji in words using a combination of hiragana and kanji use the Japanese reading, くんよみ. On the other hand, if the word is composed of two or more kanji without any hiragana, then normally the おんよみ is used. When the kanji is all by itself, your first inclination should be to use the くんよみ reading.

How Kanji is Introduced

The following key shows the sections of each new kanji introduced.

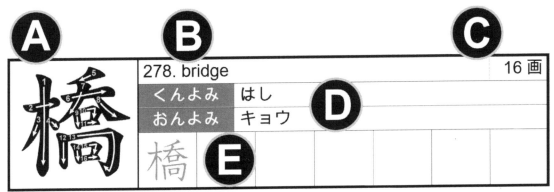

New Kanji Key

Ⓐ Kanji Stroke Order

Ⓑ Kanji Number & English Meaning

Ⓒ Stroke Count (画 is read as かく)

Ⓓ The Official Kanji Readings

Ⓔ Kanji Writing Practice Boxes

Ⓕ Kanji Words

Lesson 25: Kanji 一二三四五

New Kanji あたらしい かんじ

Make sure you learn the correct stroke order. Correct stroke order will mean neater symbols when writing quickly. Also, take time to learn the words listed for each kanji – these will help you memorize the different readings.

1. one		1 画
くんよみ	ひと (つ)	
おんよみ	イチ、イツ	

one time	one thing	January	unification
いち ど	ひと	いち がつ	とう いつ
一度	一つ	一月	統一

2. two		2 画
くんよみ	ふた (つ)	
おんよみ	ニ	

two things	February	2nd of the month	2nd floor
ふた	に がつ	ふつ か	に かい
二つ	二月	二日	二階

	3. three			3 画
	くんよみ	みっ (つ)		
	おんよみ	サン		
	三			

triangle	third dimension	3rd of the month	three things
さんかく	さん じ げん	みっ か	みっ
三角	三次元	三日	三つ

	4. four			5 画
	くんよみ	よっ (つ)		
	おんよみ	シ、ヨン		
	四			

April	four	square	four things
よ じ	よん	し かく	よっ
四時	四	四角	四つ

	5. five			4 画
	くんよみ	いつ (つ)		
	おんよみ	ゴ		
	休			

five things	5th day of month	five senses	five minutes
いつ	いつ か	ご かん	ご ふん
五つ	五日	五感	五分

Writing Points かくポイント

❑ Numbers in kanji versus "1, 2, 3…"

In modern Japan, kanji numbers are not used as frequently as in the past. More commonly, numbers are written with Arabic numerals (1, 2, 3…). One factor that probably influenced this was the limitation of early computers. Written Japanese employs many more characters than English and accordingly requires a more sophisticated computer code. It would have been more convenient to use Arabic numerals for computing, and the practice probably stuck.

Although there is still a place for kanji numbers in Japan, they aren't used as frequently today. In Japan today you will see the Arabic numbers you are used to on TV, clocks, license plates and just about anything that uses numbers. However you do need to know the number kanji since many words and phrases integrate these kanji into them.

Words You Can Write かける ことば

一つ（ひとつ） one thing

一	つ								

一時（いちじ） one o'clock

一	じ								

二個（にこ） two things (small / round objects)

二	こ								

二つ（ふたつ） two things (general objects)

二	つ								

二日 (ふつか) 2nd day of the month

二	つ								

三つ (みっつ) three things

三	つ								

三日 (みっか) 3rd day of the month

三	か								

四つ (よっつ) four things

四	つ								

四時 (よじ) four o'clock

四	じ								

四駆 (よんく) four wheel drive

四	く								

五つ (いつつ) five things

五	つ								

五時 (ごじ) five o'clock

五	じ								

三月 (さんがつ) March

三	が	つ					

四月 (しがつ) April

四	が	つ					

Word Practice ことばの れんしゅう

Fill in the appropriate kanji in the blanks for each sentence.

1. あした ＿＿＿じ＿＿＿じゅう＿＿＿ふんに ひろごはんを たべます。
   （いち）（よん）　　　　（ご）

   Tomorrow I will eat lunch at 1:45.

2. かみが ＿＿＿まいと えんぴつが ＿＿＿ほん、あります。
   （さん）　　　　　　　（に）

   There are 3 sheets of paper and 2 pencils.

3. ＿＿＿がつ＿＿＿かの＿＿＿じに いきます。
   （に）　（みっ）（よ）

   I will go on February 3rd at 4 o'clock.

4. おとうさんは ＿＿＿じゅう＿＿＿さいです。
   （ご）　　　　（いっ）

   Father is 51 years old.

5. わたしは まいにち コーラを ＿＿＿ぽん のみます。
   （いっ）

   I drink one bottle of cola everyday.

6. にほんに ともだちが ＿＿＿にん います。
   （ご）

   I have 5 friends in Japan.

7. たなかさんは ＿＿＿じ＿＿＿じゅっぷんごろ とうちゃくします。
   （に）　（よん）

   Takana san will arrive around 2:45.

8. こどもたちが ＿＿＿かくと ＿＿＿かくを ＿＿＿つ かきました。
   （さん）　　　（し）　　　（いっ）

   The children drew 5 triangles and squares.

Kanji Practice Sheet れんしゅう

Hiragana Cards

The next few pages can be cut out to make flash cards. Or you can just flip back and forth to see if you know the hiragana character.

あ	か	が
い	き	ぎ
う	く	ぐ
え	け	げ
お	こ	ご

ga	ka	a
gi	ki	i
gu	ku	u
ge	ke	e
go	ko	o

さ	ざ	た
し	じ	ち
す	ず	つ
せ	ぜ	て
そ	ぞ	と

ta	za	sa
chi	ji	shi
tsu	zu	su
te	ze	se
to	zo	so

だ	な	は
ぢ	に	ひ
づ	ぬ	ふ
で	ね	へ
ど	の	ほ

ha	na	da
hi	ni	ji
fu	nu	zu
he	ne	de
ho	no	do

ば	ぱ	ま
び	ぴ	み
ぶ	ぷ	む
べ	ぺ	め
ぼ	ぽ	も

ma	pa	ba
mi	pi	bi
mu	pu	bu
me	pe	be
mo	po	bo

や	る	ん
ゆ	れ	きゃ
よ	ろ	きゅ
ら	わ	きょ
り	を	ぎゃ

n	ru	ya
kya	re	yu
kyu	ro	yo
kyo	wa	ra
gya	wo	ri

ぎゅ	じゃ	ちょ
ぎょ	じゅ	にゃ
しゃ	じょ	にゅ
しゅ	ちゃ	にょ
しょ	ちゅ	ひゃ

cho	ja	gyu
nya	ju	gyo
nyu	jo	sha
nyo	cha	shu
hya	chu	sho

ひゅ	ぴゃ	みょ
ひょ	ぴゅ	りゃ
びゃ	ぴょ	りゅ
びゅ	みゃ	りょ
びょ	みゅ	

myo	pya	hyu
rya	pyu	hyo
ryu	pyo	bya
ryo	mya	byu
	myu	byo

Bonus Practice Sheet れんしゅう

Katakana Cards

The next few pages can be cut out to make flash cards. Or you can just flip back and forth to see if you know the katakana character.

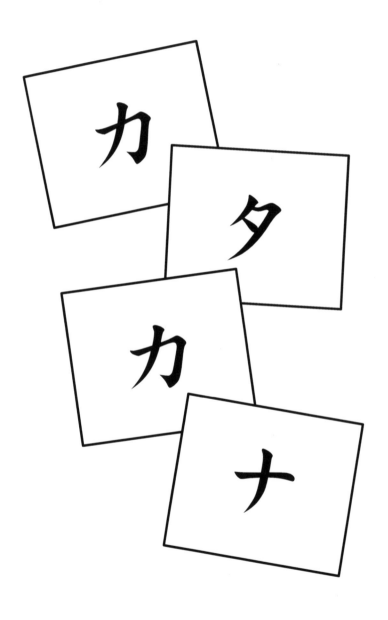

ア	カ	ガ
イ	キ	ギ
ウ	ク	グ
エ	ケ	ゲ
オ	コ	ゴ

ga	ka	a
gi	ki	i
gu	ku	u
ge	ke	e
go	ko	o

サ	ザ	タ
シ	ジ	チ
ス	ズ	ツ
セ	ゼ	テ
ソ	ゾ	ト

ta	za	sa
chi	ji	shi
tsu	zu	su
te	ze	se
to	zo	so

ダ	ナ	ハ
ヂ	ニ	ヒ
ヅ	ヌ	フ
デ	ネ	ヘ
ド	ノ	ホ

ha	na	da
hi	ni	ji
fu	nu	zu
he	ne	de
ho	no	do

バ	パ	マ
ビ	ピ	ミ
ブ	プ	ム
ベ	ペ	メ
ボ	ポ	モ

ma	pa	ba
mi	pi	bi
mu	pu	bu
me	pe	be
mo	po	bo

ヤ	ル	ン
ユ	レ	キャ
ヨ	ロ	キュ
ラ	ワ	キョ
リ	ヲ	ギャ

n	ru	ya
kya	re	yu
kyu	ro	yo
kyo	wa	ra
gya	wo	ri

ギュ	ジャ	チョ
ギョ	ジュ	ニャ
シャ	ジョ	ニュ
シュ	チャ	ニョ
ショ	チュ	ヒャ

cho	ja	gyu
nya	ju	gyo
nyu	jo	sha
nyo	cha	shu
hya	chu	sho

ヒュ	ピャ	ミョ
ヒョ	ピョ	リャ
ビャ	ピュ	リュ
ビュ	ミャ	リョ
ビョ	ミュ	ー

myo   pya   hyu

rya   pyo   hyo

ryu   pyu   bya

ryo   mya   byu

This doubles the
Katakana sound   myu   byo
that it follows

ティ	ファ	チェ
ディ	フィ	トゥ
シェ	フェ	ドゥ
ジェ	フォ	
ヴァ	ウェ	

che	fa	ti
tu	fi	di
du	fe	she
	fo	je
	we	va

Other From Zero! Books

Printed in Poland
by Amazon Fulfillment
Poland Sp. z o.o., Wrocław

65743026R10125